THE
PROBLEM

NOTES ON EVERYDAY CREATIVITY

WITH
MUSES

DAVID DUCHEMIN

CRAFT&VISION

THE PROBLEM WITH MUSES
NOTES ON EVERYDAY CREATIVITY

DAVID DUCHEMIN

www.davidduchemin.com

Editor: Cynthia Haynes
Project Manager: Corwin Hiebert

Cover Image:
Allegorical Portrait of Urania, Muse of Astronomy
by Louis Tocqué (1696-1772)
Public Domain

ISBN 978-1-7772206-2-4
First Edition, July 2020
© 2020 David duChemin

Published by Craft & Vision
A Division of Pixelated Image Communications, Inc
CraftAndVision.com

Printed in the USA

To the Muses, problematic as they are, who relentlessly bid us to make something bigger than ourselves and–in so-doing–to become bigger, ourselves, than we once were.

And to you who do the hard work of conjuring, and following, the Muses in the first place.

CONTENTS

01.
Foreword

This is a book of ideas concerning the creative life, though I hesitate to write that because all life is, or can be, creative. We are hardwired for it. Even those who don't readily identify as "creative people" find themselves facing obstacles well familiar to those whose everyday work is much more identifiable as creative work. We long to make things of our own choosing and invention, even if that thing is not a painting or a book, but the course of a career or how we run our businesses or homes; the struggles we face are universal.

This book is the written collection of the recorded episodes of my podcast, *A Beautiful Anarchy*, the title of which I stole shamelessly from my book of the same name. The through-line in these chapters is this: *you are not alone.* You are not the only one struggling to find your voice and find the courage to share what you do with the world or take creative risks. You're not the only one who looks for inspiration or direction only to find it absent, which is where the title of this book comes from; the problem with muses is that they are not something external to who we are, but are a part of who we are. The struggle to be creative is inseparable from the struggle to be. To be authentic. To be bold. To be willing to learn from failures and make hard decisions. And because creativity happens not only in our inner lives, it is also the struggle to do—to find or make the time, to fight procrastination, to finish our work, to wrestle with the many voices that clamour to be heard over the one voice that must be heard first: *our own.*

You are not alone. I have been making my living exclusively by my creative efforts for over 30 years: first a comedian, then a photographer, and now mostly a writer (though still also a photographer and an entrepreneur), a very poor guitar player and, by virtue of necessity, also a designer, publisher, and marketer. The *being* and *doing* of all these things has been an extraordinary adventure into the creative world, and in every expression of that creative urge, I have found similar joys and common struggles.

The thing I do has changed often, but the accompanying fears and obstacles are usually the same. The need for someone to be there to either call me forward or cheerlead from the sidelines has also never changed. Creativity always happens in the context of uncertainty and change, and as this book goes to print, the world is grappling with the Covid-19 pandemic and feeling that uncertainty and change more acutely than it has in a very long time. If there was ever a time we needed to be reminded that we're not alone, now must certainly be one of them. If there was ever a time we needed bold and unique thinking and not only creative ideas but creative actions, it is now. I wrote every piece in this book to strengthen, equip, and give courage to the creative spirit in all of us.

This book is not about the pandemic; it doesn't address it at all, except perhaps in passing, but I believe the pandemic will change everything. It will make clear the desperate need we have of people that live and think and act creatively. It will change the way we work, and that will require a creative and resilient response from people unafraid of change, or at least willing to courageously look change in the eye regardless of the fear. Most of all, I hope it will show us how resilient we are, even if it also reminds us that life is short and unpredictable, and that alone should push us to take more risks with our creativity and be less willing to settle for mediocrity in what we make, in our relationships, and in the day-to-day moments that, ultimately, are how we live our lives. And if all that is true, we shall need the ideas in this book all the more.

So what's the problem with muses? Seen as external sources of inspirations that we either credit with our ideas or blame when those ideas are conspicuously absent, the problem with muses is that they allow us to abdicate the choices we make and the ferocity with which we might make them if we knew and accepted that it was all up to us. But the beauty of the muses is that if you accept that they are just symbolic of that more creative side of yourself, then you need not wait for them to appear, to inspire or to embolden you. You need only be who you already are—and are becoming. Relentlessly. Generously. With a willingness to feel vulnerable and to courageously make whatever it is you make, whether that's a book, a photograph, software, a vaccine, or a business; whether it's making art or making a difference or just making a life that fits into no mold but your own.

It's my sincerest hope that the ideas in these chapters give you wisdom, courage, hope, the odd chuckle, and an abiding sense that you are neither incomplete nor alone.

David duChemin
Nanoose Bay, British Columbia
June 2020

02.
Imposter Syndrome

Among the well-worn tropes within the creative world is this: *fake it till you make it*. We've all said it. Or thought it. Particularly when we feel like we don't belong, like we have no idea what we're doing, when we feel like everyone else has their creative shit together and we're staring into the void hoping no one discovers we have no real idea what the hell we're doing. Everyone I know feels like an imposter.

Imposter syndrome is a state in which we believe not only that we're faking it, that we're not *real photographers* or *real artists* (or whatever discipline you work within) but wannabes and fakes. And it's the belief that no one else feels this way, especially those we look up to. We mistakenly believe that they have their shit together. That they are as confident on the inside as they look on the outside. I'm here to tell you, they are as full of shit as we are. And not just full of it, but it's not even together, per se. Like you and me, their shit is wildly disorganized and crammed into whatever little mental cranny is available to make it all look tidy. But it's not.

Imposter syndrome is a symptom of comparing yourself to others. We only feel like fakes because we're looking at others (all of whom also feel like fakes in some way) and measuring *our insides* against *their outsides*. We look at ourselves through a cracked and grimy mirror and at others through recently cleaned stained glass, usually rose-coloured. The comparisons are profoundly unfair.

We are *all* faking it. But that's not a bad thing. Not when faking it means *making it up as we go*. Learning what it means to be us. To be alive in this world and to create whatever it is we make as our art from that place of vulnerability and humility.

We aren't faking who we are. We're not pretending about that, and we're not trying to be something we aren't; we're just making our art with both feet planted firmly in uncertainty. Uncertain of the future, of the thing we're making—the photographs, bodies of work, writing, whatever—and uncertain of how we feel about it. That's a short list of the near infinite uncertainties we have.

Uncertainty keeps us humble. It keeps us asking questions. It keeps us hungry for more, for better, for deeper. Uncertainty is the natural habitat of the artist (which is shorthand for human being). The only thing we really know for sure is what we would discover on the well-worn paths that most artists avoid for fear of repeating themselves.

In other words, the good stuff is in the uncertainty. The uncertainty is what lies on the other side of the comfort zone. It's where the magic (if there is such a thing) is to be found.

Uncertainty is not, however, the same as a lack of confidence or a lack of courage. It is the *reason* we need those very things. Confidence in the creative process to get us where we're going without the map we wish we had. Courage to begin, to do, to make, to move forward, knowing that the way is dark, that we might bump into things, but that bumping into things has never yet truly harmed us. And when we don't have confidence or courage, to pretend we do and get to work all the same. Courage isn't that rare state of being in which we have no fear: it's the will to act regardless and not be *paralyzed* by our fear.

The initial intent of this chapter was to encourage you, but I feel myself sliding into a sermon to try to convince your mind that it's all a game when what I want most to do is to speak to your heart.

So listen up, you deeper parts in which the doubt and the fears reside: the greatest artists and creative people against which you could possibly compare yourselves were a hot, sticky mess. They were truly messy, troubled, long-suffering souls. No artist in the history of time has had their shit together any more than you do.

A short list of brilliant people who most decidedly did not have their shit together: Picasso, Ernest Hemingway, Sylvia Plath, Vincent van Gogh, Tennessee Williams, Kurt Cobain, Beethoven, Georgia O'Keeffe, Goya, Caravaggio, Freddie Mercury, and probably anyone who's ever appeared on the cover of *Rolling Stone* magazine. Messy, troubled, mercurial, even broken? Perhaps. But aren't we all? To quote Leonard Cohen (another bright mess of a human being), aren't those the cracks where the light gets in?

I've long believed that our comfort zones are not where our best art is made and not remotely where our best lives are lived. There are all kinds of reasons we camp out in those comfort zones, but if it's the so-called imposter syndrome keeping you there, then it's time to take a deeper look at who you keep comparing yourself against. Not at the brave face they put on for the public, not their Instagram feeds and their Facebook posts, but the soul-level things. We are all afraid. We all live looking forward into uncertainty (unless you live looking backward, and that's arguably worse).

For however else you and I differ from each other and from the great creative people of history, we share that we are broken, messy people, dogged by fears and traumas, buoyed now and then by hopes and joys. And when we accomplish any great and beautiful thing—at whatever scale we make it—it is not made because we lack fear or possess remarkable genes; it is because in all our human weakness, and from the middle of stories fraught with complications, we do the work and pour ourselves into it.

It is not from raw talent nor from privileged lives that art comes, but from a willingness to splash that humanity, however messy and uncertain, onto the canvas, write it into the story, or put it into the photograph.

We may have a lot of reasons for not making our art or doing the work. But it is not (and must never be) that others have it easier, are more talented, or in any other way have their shit together more than we do. It is a profoundly human state of being to lack shit-togetherness. The imposter, if there is one at all, is not the one whose life is a disorganized mess; it's the one who fails to recognize it, accept it, and get back to work. Flaws and all. You don't need to fake it. You just need to be you.

You might not be the smartest person in the world. Only one person can hold that title. I sure as hell don't.

Make your art anyway.

You might not be able to do it all by yourself; few of us can. I can't.

Make your art anyway.

You might not be as talented as you think others are. Talent is overrated and most often just the result of hard work; you just don't see the effort, only the results. Results always look easy.

Make your art anyway.

You might think you have had it too easy, or too hard. You haven't.

Make your art.

Make *your* art.

You do that by being you and no one else. The only imposter is the one trying to be someone else.

We don't need you to be someone else—someone shiny, unbroken, or, for that matter, to be a dark and tortured genius. We don't need you to have your shit together. We just need you to be relentlessly and unapologetically you.

And to make your art.

And because making that art always happens in the uncertainty of new and unfamiliar territory, every step forward is on ground on which you've never stepped. Ground where you don't yet belong. If you don't feel you belong it's because, in a very real sense, you don't. You've just arrived. And any time you feel you do belong, you're probably due to move on and stop wearing a rut into the carpet. By the time you pay your dues, you'll be on to the next place. And let me tell you one more thing: while I truly believe there's no one out there checking your credentials to see if you belong—no guardians of any one creative space—if they are there, they've been there too long and they are not looking in the one direction that matters: toward their own work. Ignore them. You can only listen to one voice at a time and theirs is not the one that matters. You are right where you're meant to be, and you're not alone.

03.
Overwhelmed

I completely wasted the first two hours of this morning until I finally came to my senses and shook myself loose from the pull of Instagram and Facebook and the endless digital hooks that seem to catch my attention these days. And at the end of those two hours, I felt overwhelmed, absolutely swamped. I felt small in the face of it all. I not only felt uninspired but that my creative light, a flickering fragile thing at the best of times, had been doused for the day.

I hear this more and more from my friends and total strangers online alike, many of whom, like me, have taken to social media to complain about social media. And the word I keep hearing is "overwhelmed." I'm hearing it with such frequency that it's fast becoming my word for the year: eleven letters that seem to sum up the prevailing mood for me.

During my last visit to Rome, I stood in front of the great Japanese painter Hokusai's painting, *Under the Wave off Kanagawa*, often called *The Great Wave*. You'd probably recognize it if you saw it: a great tsunami of a wave on the left side of the canvas, all swirling whites and blues, about to crash down on two longboats of Japanese fishermen, dwarfed by the force of the wave above them that seems to reach out for all of them with grasping fingers while Mount

Fuji sits dwarfed in the background as if it, too, might be enveloped by the wave.

I feel Hokusai's great wave in my soul these days—the ocean moving under and over me all at once, at times threatening to swallow me whole in one overwhelming wave of obligations, overcommitment, emails, and the constant tinnitus of social media that makes it hard to hear anything else very clearly, least of all my own voice.

I don't think we're hardwired to be able to deal with this much information, this many so-called friends, fans, followers and likes and news clips from corners of the globe we are powerless to change. Our hearts and minds aren't large enough to contain, much less filter, the many voices and images we absorb. And if you're a creative person, seeing the flood of other people's work, their successes and awards, and being exposed to a volume of thoughts and chatter that no generation on the planet has ever had to deal with; it's just too much raging water through pipes too small. It's too much noise.

It is, in the truest sense of the word, overwhelming. To be overwhelmed is to be submerged completely, so it's no wonder Hokusai's Great Wave provides (at least for me) a powerful visual metaphor. What makes the painting even stronger is that the wave never falls. It hangs there day after day, in permanent tension and threat, and the rowers haven't made a foot of progress in the last 200 years. They are still there, assumingly terrified of the wave and the threat of washing them away entirely. That, I think, is the worst of it. And it's what I fear most about the threat of being overwhelmed in my own life: not so much that the one rogue wave is coming, but that the fear of it will keep me cowering, and if not cowering, then *paralyzed*.

The most fulfilling moments in my creative life have been the moments where I am moving forward, exploring new things, chasing some idea that just seems to be *right*, right now. That's when I'm in the flow. The great wave is not flow; it's flood. It's uncontrollable and unsustainable and too big to do anything with. It makes a great metaphor, but it's lousy if I want to accomplish anything. Flow is the opposite. It's focused and smooth and, yes, sometimes it feels a little too fast, like it might get away on us, but when it happens you never feel like you're so in control, or maybe that it's in control of you sometimes but it's benevolent and exciting and you can't wait to see where it's leading. On the other hand, the great wave almost always seems to lead to the shore, where if we aren't dashed onto the rocks, we're stranded on the beach wondering where we are and what the hell just happened.

I've got another water metaphor, but first, let me say why I think this all matters. I have never, not once, made anything good—a photograph or a piece of writing, or some other more mundane creative output—when I've been paralyzed by the overwhelm. I just freeze up, my eyes going to the top of the wave and holding there. And if I do act, if I shake myself free from it, there's a good chance I'm just frantically bailing out the boat. Reply to email, post to Instagram, get busy doing the million things that make up our daily lives and seem to guarantee that the wave will always hover.

Back to the metaphor. What if all this is more within our control than we accept? What if we have the ability to turn the water off at the source? To close the browser, to put the phone away, and disengage from social media if that's what's overwhelming you? What if all this talk of being overwhelmed, as real and scary as it can be, is just a result of abdicating our agency, our choices, as human beings? When did we forget what the world was like before Facebook, and days carved into thinner and thinner slices by anyone and everyone who asks for a piece? When did we stop saying *no*?

Current means of communication tend to just be a pipe with no faucet; the water just keeps coming, often unsolicited. And there we are at the end of it, knowing it's too much—that our bucket isn't big enough, and looking frantically for a bigger bucket. I don't think there's a bucket big enough, and still, it comes.

Years ago, I wrote a book called *Within The Frame: The Journey of Photographic Vision*. To my great delight, it became a best-seller, such as best-sellers are in the small world of popular photography. Suddenly I was inundated with emails and invitations to speak, and the gentle flow of water that had been my creative and business life was suddenly coming out of the pipes so hard I had no idea what to do with it. I was completely overwhelmed. For a while, I loved it, but then it was just too much. Emails I once welcomed were suddenly mixed with angry missives from people who wondered why I hadn't replied to them and just who the hell did I think I was that I couldn't just take a moment to say thank you for the kind words or answer their question? I hadn't asked for their email, hadn't known that it would be only a drop in a bucket of *hundreds* of emails, and I didn't have the time to reply to enough of them to make the slightest difference. The blessing very quickly became a curse.

I think many of the things in our lives that overwhelm us do so because they start out so good. So small. They seem manageable, even exciting. But like so many things, they get bigger, taking on a life of their own. The wave builds. How many of us started down the social media road with even the remotest of ideas that it was so intentionally designed to be addictive? Truly, scientifically, addictive. How many of us have any idea when we commit to the things we do that they'll take so much time, go off the rails, or become an emotional drain? Life has this habit of sneaking up on us; in the freelance world, we call it "scope creep." You agree to do something for a client for X amount and, if you let it happen, it's not long before tiny little tweaks and changes happen to the scope of work. An addition here, a redo there, a quick favour that takes us half a day. Scope creep always, always builds, until one day, we're treading water and wondering how it all just got so out of control as it knocks us from the boat.

When the success of my first book proved too much to handle, I felt like I was on the edge of a meltdown. My bandwidth was monopolized by this new flood of attention and work and all the things that come with that (things that I'm truly, deeply grateful for) but have had to learn to control. I was forced to find strategies that would help me free up that bandwidth because it's not enough just to learn to deal with the new level of demands. If my entire world becomes dealing with those demands, if that becomes my work, then when do I do my real work? When do I make my photographs? When do I write my next book or next article? When do I find the margins of silence and solitude that I need to even contemplate the deeper work? And what about the relationships that fill the well to do that work? When will I find time for those?

Ultimately, this is about resource management, specifically the very limited resources of *time* and *attention*. Those are the buckets that are consistently filled to overflowing, and the buckets aren't getting any bigger because our stores of time and attention aren't increasing. We have what we have. And many of us are squandering them as if they're limitless, and that is where the overwhelm comes from.

It isn't my intention to tell you how to deal with the flood of things that overwhelm you, though I have some ideas. I think many of us just need to know we're not alone, that it's a shared struggle, and to understand that we are in control, or we can be if we'll wrestle that control back from those to whom we've accidentally relinquished it. What I'd like to do is leave you with the same questions I've been asking myself in my struggle to claw back my resources so they're available to me to do my best work, so I have wider margins and more breathing room, so I have time to not only do my work, but my *best* and deeper work, as well as to live my best life.

What would happen if you recognized how scarce and limited your time and attention were? How would your life change if you realized that saying yes to all the trivial things—the ad hoc obligations and scope creep—was the same as saying no to the most important things in your life?

How long are you going to wait before you start saying yes to the right things, the best things, and no to the rest?

What would happen if you tracked your time this week? What changes would you make if you realized you'd spent six hours on Facebook—six hours of your life with which you might have done something more meaningful?

How can you buy back the margins in your life, reclaim some of your mental bandwidth?

How would your life change if you stopped watching the news and focused instead on the lives you *could* change instead of working yourself into a lather about those you could not? Surely our empathy isn't limitless, either.

And practically speaking, what would you do with the six hours of your week that you could buy back by paying the neighbour kid to mow the lawn, shovel the driveway, or by hiring someone to clean the house?

There are ways to reverse the scope creep, dial back the obligations, and take control of what makes demands on our attention. We are not passive players in this life. There are enough things, both good and bad, that we can't control that will rock our worlds and send us to our knees: a pregnancy, a diagnosis, a layoff, an unexpected success, the passing of people we never imagined our worlds without. Making art, whatever that means to you, has always been a way of navigating those deeper waters, a way of experiencing them more fully, coping with them, and making sense of them. But we can't do that while paralyzed under the great wave.

04.
Be Very You

Your first task as an artist (or whatever you choose to call yourself if the word "artist" gives you hives) is to be *you*. Not reluctantly, not hesitantly, and not in half-measures, though that's how it often starts. Your first task is not to figure out what "art" means or to have an exhibit, write a book, or get business cards that say "artist" on them. It's to be (and to become) *you*.

On the most basic level, you are all you have as an artist. By that, I mean you are the one thing you have that no one else does. Others may have years of expertise in whatever craft or crafts you have chosen to practice, but they do not have *you*. They don't have your taste, your opinions, your background, your stories, or any of the other things that make you uniquely you.

"You" is not something you look for or find; it's something you own. I don't mean you possess it, but that you *accept* it, without apology for the rough edges and the ways you don't match the template, or how the squishy bits overflow the mold into which we are all made to feel we should easily fit.

The best artists in history (those who made art with their lives, on canvases of many different kinds) share only one thing: they were boldly themselves and no one else. Monet,

Picasso, Kahlo, and Warhol asked no one for permission to follow their whims, their muses, their own voices.

Nor did David Bowie, Stephen Hawking, Emily Dickinson, or Tony Bourdain. They were simply focused on being exactly who they were and, so far as we know, didn't lose a moment's sleep on trying to be anyone else, trying on anyone else's voice, or asking permission from others to be very much themselves.

It is only from that place of defiant you-ness that you will change the world, even if you think your world is just you and the kids and you have no designs on changing the big picture. But if you do want to change the big picture, it had better start with you; only then do the ripples of impact fan out to touch others, in whatever measure you dream of.

What the world needs is not more polite deference, not more doing what we *ought* to do, or saying what we *ought* to say, but a million voices saying and doing precisely what life has put in their hearts and minds and saying and doing those things at the top of our lungs and our lives.

We do not need more blending in so we all reach the grave looking as much like one another on the outside as we do on the inside, all filled with the same regrets for never having been the one person we could have been with our one beautiful short life: *ourselves*.

It is that one person being defiantly themselves who will change the world. When I refer to a beautiful anarchy in the title of my podcast, those are the people I mean—not the ones burning tires in the streets, but the ones living life on their terms, doing what others say can't be done and, where necessary, doing what "shouldn't" be done.

They're the ones from whom we get courage; the ones who inspire change; the ones who offer hope and kick at the darkness to let the light in.

They are the ones who speak the truth to power, ask the unwelcome but much-needed questions, and defend the little guy or the one born to this culture (or freshly arrived at the doorsteps of "our" countries) with the "wrong" gender or skin colour or believing the "wrong" things.

They are the ones who will say yes when the rest say no and (perhaps harder) say no when the rest say yes.

You can only do that if you are being you and no one else. That is the task of the artist: not to blend in but to stand out. And from there, to paint your hope, your light, your questions, even your warnings (because what were the prophets of old if not defiantly themselves, and what is this planet now if not in need of change?).

What the world needs now, as I suppose it always has, is for us to stop playing small.

We could change the world and yet we're scrapping in the dirt for Instagram likes. There are people with millions of followers, more than Jesus Christ Himself had, and they're shilling for teeth whiteners while the planet heads towards the boiling point and politics everywhere slide with terrifying speed toward nationalism, fascism, and the marginalization of those who are different.

We need hope.

We need light.

We need people to play to their strengths and not to the crowd.

That is what it has always meant to be an artist. I care less about defining the word "art" than I care to speculate about how many angels can dance on the head of a pin, but I know it comes from people who have something to say—people with the courage to be themselves and no one else and then to implore us to do the same. Forget trying to be an artist; forget whether or not the thing you make with your life is art or not. It doesn't matter. Just be as profoundly, defiantly, unwaveringly you as you can. If that's not art, I don't know what is.

And before you give yourself an out on this one because you're "just one person" or "not really an artist," I want to remind you that everyone who ever made a bit of difference in this world was "just one person" and everyone who ever made anything (whether their art was on canvas, in the political arena, or scientific research) started out as "not really an artist"—just humans leaning into being the one thing they could be better than anyone else: themselves.

This is not a call to arms. It's not a manifesto. It's a reminder of the humble but outrageous job description of the artist: to be fully ourselves. Don't settle. Don't shy away. Don't flinch when you look in the mirror. Whatever other messages you hear that tell you that you aren't smart enough, pretty enough, thin enough, strong enough, young enough, or old enough are wrong. You've got everything you need to be you, and from that place of being, to make and do your art.

Whatever else you do today, be very, very you.

05.
Leaving Dafen

There is a village in China where thousands of painters make their living together, painting away their days in spartan studios, covered in colourful smears and splatters, surrounded by canvases. The village is called Dafen, and it intrigues me because, for all the technical prowess possessed by the painters in that community, it is not known for its *art*. Not really. That is to say it's not known for its *own* art; it's known for being the world's largest source of counterfeits and copies of art. Want to own the *Mona Lisa* but don't have the 500 million it might cost you? You can get one in Dafen for a handful of dollars, relatively speaking. And it'll be a *very* good copy. But is it art? Was it made by an artist? Why does it matter?

Hypothetical questions about what is or isn't art don't interest most everyday creative people. We'd rather just do what we do and let others decide if it's art, and I'm with you on that—sort of.

If art is more than just technique and imitation, no matter how perfect that imitation, then it requires something more than just years of practice. It requires *us*. It requires interpretation. It requires that we bring something of our own to the table, preferably something that means something to us, something that's a part of us. It requires vulnerability and soul and thoughts of our own. It takes courage.

Metaphorically, I spent several years living in Dafen. I believe many (if not most) artists who require some level of competency of craft do the same. We learn our trade there; we take the first steps to mastering our craft there. And if that's all we want, we can spend our lives there, happily copying the ideas and art of others with increasing perfection. The paintings will get better with time. But they will not come any closer to being *yours*.

If you want to get exceptionally good at your craft, stay in Dafen. If you're a photographer, go where every other photographer is going. Do what they are doing. Put your tripods in their holes in Iceland and the Faroe Islands. Make yet another photograph of Antelope Canyon or Half Dome that is indistinguishable from the previous ones. You could become extraordinarily skillful in your craft. But it won't be art; it won't be more than just a copy until you leave Dafen. The same is true of any craft that can become art the moment you put *yourself* into it.

I suspect many of the craftsmen who live in Dafen do so for much of their lives—that they make a living there and find joy in other things. I'm not for a moment trivializing that, if that's enough for them. And it might be; the painters in Dafen are *extraordinarily* good at their craft.

I'm speaking to those who keep putting their brushes to the canvas and wishing with all their souls that they could bring their own thoughts and ideas to the work they create; to those who want to explore something more with their paint, who want so badly to try things their way and see if it sticks.

Maybe you have no idea if what you make is art and you don't care, but you know you long for it to be distinctly *yours*. If that's you, I think it's probably important to recognize the danger of a place where we tend to camp out and make more of the same because it's safe and requires little more than that we strive for excellence of craft or some version of perfect. There's a danger, even when we're not copying the work of others but copying ourselves, in repeating what we've done in the past because it requires no risk on our part, except the risk of never moving forward.

Leaving Dafen is not easy, not in this metaphor. There's no bus to another province. No clearly marked path from the imitation stage where we all cut our teeth and learn our craft. But it's necessary if what you want in this one short life is to do something other than what others are doing, and instead to paint outside the lines with the blazing colours of your own choosing.

It takes one thing to leave Dafen: *courage*. But where will you go? I have no idea. What will you paint if not the Monets and the Dalis and Turners that you've imitated over and over? I haven't a clue. But whatever it is, it'll be *yours*. There will be wide margins for error and experimentation and exploration, which is frightening to anyone who's never made so much as an imperfect brush stroke. It doesn't take courage to paint by numbers, to do as we're told, or to serve our social media audiences with more of the same stuff for which we know we'll be rewarded the dopamine hit of likes and benign comments. It does take courage to go the other way, to trust your own instinct, to do more than what is expected. To write what you *feel* and not what you *ought* to say. To open yourself up to the world through your art by saying, "Here it is—here *I* am; take it or leave it," knowing that far more people than not will choose to leave it. You can't please seven billion people, nor should you try. But you can please yourself.

There's something different about you, as there is with all of us. Probably something that kids at school saw right away and teased you about; kids have a way of finding that thing that makes us different. And now there's a good chance you've spent considerable effort to hide whatever it is from the world. Whatever it is (or maybe it's a collection of things), it's the weird-shaped edges you keep trying to iron out, but they're part of you; they're there for good, so they keep springing back. They're the things that make you feel a bit like a freak. By definition, they're also what make you extraordinary. Exceptional. Sure, they made childhood a little tough, but as my friend James Victore wisely observes, it's the things that made us weird as kids that make us great as adults.

We're all trying so hard to blend in that we have no chance at standing out. And that's a shame because if you just let your freak flag fly, you'd find it was that very thing to which people were the most attracted. The real you. The messy you. The you who had the courage to leave Dafen and try it your way. Not just to be different or contrary, but to be you. Imperfect, weird, intriguing, fantastically human *you*. The kind of person who makes art, not copies: someone who is truly him or herself and not a copy of someone else.

Practice your craft with all the skill you can muster, but if you want to make more than skilled copies of something you've seen before, then you've got to do it your way—and figuring that out is a messy business. Don't camp out on craft and copy if you long for more. Don't settle. And whatever you do, don't get too comfortable, because that comfort zone is the place where creativity goes to die, where we lose momentum and forget what it feels like to experience the frisson of trying something new, being a little less apologetically ourselves, and exploring unfamiliar ideas. It's on that less-comfortable ground and in that uncertainty, far from the metaphorical Dafen, where not only are we able to make our art, but our art begins to make us. Art is about transformation, and nothing will change us into the people we are becoming like the courage to make art that is yours, and yours alone.

I don't often do disclaimers, but I feel it's needed here. Dafen is a real place, driven by real economics where real people labour with great skill. I am using Dafen purely as a metaphor and in the knowledge that in the real world, we do what we must to put food on the table. This chapter in no way seeks to deny those realities, nor do I mean to imply that there might not be those in Dafen who are doing their own thing, living life on their terms and creating art. But as a metaphor, I think it's helpful to imagine a place where imitation is the norm and to understand the courage it takes to leave that place if you long for more. I hope you'll forgive me if I have oversimplified that metaphor in the interest of making my point.

06.
Just an Amateur?

I talked to an artist recently who expressed the feeling that because his art-making didn't make money for him or his family, that it felt frivolous and self-indulgent, and worse, that his family seemed to feel the same way. I've talked frequently to others who feel that because they aren't professionals they aren't "real artists." And when asked about their art, they start shuffling their feet and looking for the exit because the word we use for those who are not professionals is *amateur*, which makes it sound like we don't take this as seriously and aren't as skilled as those who whose art is also their trade. To be an amateur seems to imply an incompleteness.

If I were to guess, I'd say that most you reading this book do not rely on your art-making or creativity to pay the bills. Most of you are not, in the most literal use of the word, professionals and are, therefore, amateurs. I think that's a *good* thing.

For a word that means "to do something for the love of it," I have no idea why the word amateur gets such a bad rap. For that matter, I'm not sure why *professional* has come to be so valued, especially in the world of creativity and art-making, the one context in which you would think doing something only for the money might be eyed with more suspicion—even cynicism.

To set those of you who *do* make all or part of your living from your creativity at ease, I have no intention of putting a negative spin on being a so-called professional. I make my living from my creativity and have done so for almost 30 years. I love what I do. There are good reasons not to go down this road—perils that come with the territory—but there's no reason why you can't do this as a professional and never for a moment stop doing it for the love of it.

But it's also important that we collectively remember that the word "professional" doesn't for a moment imply that what we make is better than those who fit their art-making into the margins created by other jobs and the concerns of day-to-day life. The fact that others pay for our art—that money changes hands—can certainly be one way of feeling like what we make (and therefore we ourselves) is validated. But it's no more a sign that the work is necessarily especially good than the fact that someone greenlit the *Sharknado* movies—six times! And they've made more money than Pixar. For those doing the math, in 2017, that was over 4.5 *billion* dollars. What am I saying here? I'm saying that making money only means someone paid for what we made, and it should keep us humble to know that there's also a steady market for plastic novelty dog poo.

On the flip side, there are countless stories of astonishing art from wonderful artists who were never recognized in their lifetime, and much of it from people who never made their art professionally. Some of the most wonderful art has come from people who never left their day jobs or kept them long into their other careers as writers, composers, or other kinds of creative work. Anthony Trollope became one of the most popular and prolific authors in Victorian England while working for the post office. Franz Kafka was an insurance clerk. Harper Lee was an airline ticketing agent. Agatha Christie wrote on the side while working as a pharmacist's assistant. Kurt Vonnegut did several things, including running a car dealership, while he wrote. Herman Melville was a deputy customs inspector. Modern artist Jeff Koons, having twice broken the record for creating the most expensive work by a living artist sold at auction, was a commodities broker while he made much of his art.

Composer and artist Philip Glass continued to work as a taxi driver and plumber throughout his career. On one occasion, he was installing a dishwasher in the New York home of Robert Hughes, the art critic of *Time* magazine, who said, "But you're Philip Glass! What are you doing here?" Glass replied that he was an artist, but also sometimes a plumber, and that he needed to finish his work.

It would be easy to look at this list of people and point to their eventual commercial success as validation, but that's only something we see in hindsight. My point is that while they were making their art, they were so-called amateurs.

No one would read *Moby Dick* and say, "Well, it's a great novel; it's too bad Herman never became a 'real' writer," or "Imagine how much better the poetry of T.S. Eliot might have been if he hadn't been a bank clerk?"

There is an incredible freedom available to those who pursue their craft and make their art free from the need to make it saleable—not the least of which is the ability to make it exactly the thing you want it to be. It is that effort, borne from love and whatever other compulsions drive us to create, that fuel us and keep us making things that are authentic, that give us joy, help us find meaning. J.K. Rowling didn't write *Harry Potter* because a publisher was breathing down her neck; she wrote it for reasons all her own. It was only her work as an amateur that allowed her to later do it for a living—a choice, one assumes, she was absolutely free to make or not make once the money started coming in. Rowling's net worth is now over $1 billion, much of that made from her "amateur" efforts.

I want to go back to the artist I mentioned at the beginning of this chapter because the idea that his creative efforts were deemed less important because they didn't make him money, or that they were self-indulgent, drives me crazy. Couldn't we all use a little more self-indulgence if it leads us to do the things that fill our souls and give us meaning or joy? Wouldn't we all be happier people with richer, deeper lives? Wouldn't that add to the intangible bottom lines for the people who live with us? To look at our creative efforts as unimportant is to overlook the inescapable truth that as much as we make our art, our art also makes us. To see the work of becoming the most we can be as frivolous is to devalue our emotional and mental well-being.

Being an amateur is no reason for anyone, most especially ourselves, to take our creative work less seriously. There is no shame in being an amateur and doing something because you love it. You can't be *merely* an amateur because there is nothing *mere* about love. But there's something else—more of a kick in the pants than a hug—and that's this: you can't control whether others see your work as important, but you can control how important your work is to you.

If there's a downside to being a creative professional (and I think there are several), there is also a downside to doing it in the margins as a so-called amateur. The danger is in leaving it in the margins, giving it mere crumbs of time with any leftover energy you may have for it. Doing something for the love of it, being an amateur, in no way means that what you do should not be a priority. We prioritize what we love.

Doing it for the love of it doesn't mean it won't take the same discipline and struggle as those whose art-making also happens to be their job, though I fear many of you have been made to feel that this is so. If anything, the harder task is to make your art while other activities make your income. In other words, none of us are off the hook.

Doing it for the love of it doesn't mean you can't intentionally carve out the time to write your play. It doesn't mean that you shouldn't take seriously the need to sign your work and put it into the world in whichever ways you long to do so.

It does not in any way mean you must approach your work like a dilettante or a dabbler. Your art should not be getting the scraps of your time, energy, focus, or love; it's too important to you. And it's too important to us. We need you to be fully present in your art-making. We need to see the world the way you see it, to be inspired by your work. We need you to remind us what it looks like to go all in and not hold back.

But most of all, *you* need it; for all the reasons you make art in the first place, you need it. There was a reason you picked up that paintbrush, pen, or camera—a scratch that your creativity itches, a hollow place that it fills, or questions that it helps you find answers to. And not a bit of it has to do with anyone else or the label that you put on those efforts.

Just an amateur? I don't think so. You can do your art part-time, but you can't do it half-heartedly. Whatever you're making, wherever the muse is leading you, go all in. It might not be your job, but it's still your work.

07.
Going Deeper

I recently sat down in my chair to write, to start a new chapter in the growing pile of words that I'm kind of hoping becomes my next book. When I looked up, a couple of hours had passed, and I was 2,000 words closer to knowing where that book was taking me. It doesn't always go this well. Often the flow doesn't come, blocked by distractions and too much getting in my own way. But I'm learning to get more reliably into the flow and get my work more quickly into the deeper waters.

The work of most creative people runs the gamut, from the necessary but rather shallow trivial day-to-day tasks to the vital and deep—the things we hope might endure. That gamut includes everything from emptying the dishwasher to posting to Instagram to going to Staples to buy more pens to sitting down to write or locking yourself into the studio so you can work on your latest photographs. Much of it (like the emails and the need to update your Etsy store or blog) isn't exactly what we dream about when we think about the work of creating. It's necessary, but if we're not careful, it can dam up the river and block the flow. We could spend our lives in the shallows.

Where I think we get into trouble is when we mistake the necessary but shallow efforts for the real work of making our art; if we're not confusing one with the other, we're letting one get in the way of the other.

Last year, I noticed something had started to go off-kilter in my work life. It was a slow shift away from my most important work, the work I hope one day to be part of my legacy: my photography and, increasingly, my writing. But that work was getting pushed aside by an avalanche of lots of little things. Many of them good, but none of them very deep.

What I've learned is that our most important work, the deep work, doesn't happen accidentally in the margins of our lives, but in larger chunks. Chunks that are substantial enough for flow to happen; big enough that we have room to make mistakes and redirect our efforts. In other words, we need time to take that work past the obvious and into deep waters. We need blocks of time, not slivers. But I can sit for two hours and get an astonishing amount of nothing done. We also need focus and solitude.

Focus is a resource that's getting harder and harder to protect as more and more demands are made on us, and as we allow ourselves to fragment our attention into smaller and smaller pieces. Despite a rash of articles citing so-called research over the last ten years, our attention spans, or our capacity to pay attention, are not getting shorter. But the things we are trying to pay attention to are growing as fast as our continued belief in our ability to multi-task and deal meaningfully with several things at once, despite the real, actual research that shows we can't. More to the point, there is no such thing as productive multi-tasking.

There is no shortage of obstacles to living a fulfilling, productive, creative life, and if we're being honest, many of our obstacles are self-inflicted. The need to get a lot of things done drives many of us to multi-task, asking our brains to do something they don't have the capacity for, splitting our attention and not only getting less done, but sabotaging our ability to do better creative work. I know this because in an effort to prove that multi-tasking *could* be done, I did some research and kept bumping into hard evidence that proved otherwise; I ultimately realized I was getting a lot done, but not as well as I knew it could be. It was becoming quantity over quality, and that's not what I want my legacy to be.

Multi-tasking or attention-splitting of any kind has serious adverse effects, not only on our work, but on ourselves. A 2011 study from the University of California San Francisco showed that multi-tasking negatively affects our short-term memory. It also leads to loss of focus and anxiety and an increased inability to think creatively; multi-tasking prevents us from getting into a state of flow and causes us to make more mistakes and be less productive. In other words, you *can* multi-task, but it's killing your ability to do your best work. Your deeper work is suffering.

It might be time to kill the distractions and treat your attention like the valuable and limited resource that it is in creative work. I'm still learning to do this, but it has been a long time since I've allowed the attention-stealing notifications on my phone or laptop. When I sit down to write, I set the ringer on my phone to off before turning it over so I can't see the screen, and I write far better and longer and with more flow than I ever could with the constant notifications. Even without responding to incoming texts, calls, and emails, when we see them come in, they pull us out of flow. They make demands on our attention, and they dilute the focus we need to do our deeper work.

While I'm doing my deeper work, I find I need about two uninterrupted hours for it to be meaningful. That means no phone calls, no social media, no emails, none of those "I'll just check to see if…" moments that you look up from 45 minutes later wondering why you picked up the phone in the first place. Do it the way you need to, but know that if you want to do your *best* work, it needs to be without distraction. The brain is a wonder, but it can't deal with competing things at the same time. This is a choice we need to make with strategies that we must intentionally put into play, especially these days. By default, everything is set to maximum distraction.

The other obstacle that is increasingly prevalent is a loss of solitude. We've never been so connected. Our minds have never been so exposed to other minds. As much as we need collaboration and a variety of inputs, the loss of significant, meaningful alone time puts us at risk of losing individuality and independent thought. It's not a coincidence that the great minds of history all took great pains to do their work alone and sought solitude as a regular and uninterrupted part of their creative process.

Solitude isn't only being in a room without other people; it's being in a space where your mind isn't interacting with other minds. In other words, there's no benefit to being alone with your work if you're talking with others online or via text. The point is *focus*. If you want flow, you need focus. True solitude gives your brain time to think about your work and the problems that you are trying to solve without being pulled into the thoughts and concerns of other minds, even when you're all talking about you and your work. It gives you time to develop your ideas beyond the most obvious thoughts and solutions, to really process the thinking that will make your work a reflection of you and not merely the homogenous result of crowdsourcing.

At the risk of looking like that Luddite who's always whining about social media—the equivalent of that old guy who yells, "Get off my lawn!"—let me suggest that this is yet another area in which our *intentional* use of those tools are necessary to keep us from going off the rails.

As a photographer, this new tech makes it too easy and too tempting to make a series of photographs, do some edits, and post it all online for public consumption in less time than it used to take to rewind a roll of film and reload the camera. The same is true of writing or anything else that can be consumed digitally.

The danger is that we're asking others to weigh in with opinions on our work before we've had a chance to form our *own* opinions about that work, before we've had a chance to live with those images and react to them, allowing them to give us new ideas and direction. It takes time to know whether the image you're looking at is final or merely a sketch that will lead to stronger, deeper work. And when we put it out there—whether calling it done or not—we're neither giving ourselves nor our work the chance to incubate a while without the input of others.

Input can be good, but the kind of feedback we get when we ask the internet is always a mixed bag at best. When we ask everyone with an opinion what they think of our work, they'll tell us. But we have no idea if these people have any taste whatsoever, any experience with the creative process, or any willingness to try to understand what we're trying to accomplish before they sound off on it.

Expose your work to enough people, and the feedback will be so wildly all over the map and varied that it will be useless and give you nothing but a sense that some people like it and some people don't. That's not new, and it's not helpful.

Your most important work is your deep work. The book, the body of work, the new album, or whatever core thing you do, the biggest threat to your deep work is the shallow stuff; the little things that fill the time needed to do the bigger things. As more and more of those little things demand our attention and time and allow us the impression that getting it done is the same as doing our real work, the more possible it is that we're neglecting the bigger projects on which careers, reputations, and legacies are actually built. We could all spend a year running in circles chasing the minutiae only to get to the end of that year without accomplishing anything more than maintenance—no legacy work, nothing larger than a few really great emails and Facebook posts. No one is going to look back at their Twitter feed and their to-do lists and see it as meaningful, creative work.

When's the last time you set time aside to do your best work free from distractions? When's the last time you made it a priority and yelled, "Hold my calls!" even if that means turning the phone off yourself? Is the frustration over doing less of the work that stirs your soul and makes you happy because you've never called that work out as important, if only to you? Could it be that you've seen all the work in your creative life as equal so that what gets done are always (and only) the urgent things that clamour loudest for your attention, while the real work sits quietly in the back waiting for you to give it the time, attention, focus, and solitude that it needs? If you won't make that happen, if you won't take that work deeper, who will?

08.
The Problem with Muses

In ancient Greek mythology, there were nine muses who were responsible for the worlds of literature, science, and the arts. They were our sources of inspiration—minor goddesses who could be credited and praised for the best of our creative efforts and, I suppose, blamed when it all went to shit and nothing was flowing.

I have to admit that I'm not sure which is more appealing to me: having a muse to get me rolling or having someone to blame on the days when everything I do feels like it's not working. If I had a muse (beyond the symbolic one I spend much of my time pleading and cursing with), I suspect we'd spend most of our time in couple's therapy.

The problem with muses is that they aren't forces external to ourselves. They are neither our creative salvation nor the ones responsible for whatever version of writer's block applies to your specific creative endeavours. The problem with muses is precisely that they are us and we are them.

Our ideation, the processes that create the ideas that become our eventual creative output, is entirely an internal thing. It's a function of the brain. I don't understand much more than that on a scientific level, but I do know that the implications are exciting for those of us who rely on the way we think to make our art, make a living, or both.

Accepting that we are the source of our own ideas and that we have the responsibility for the care and feeding of the muse means we can reliably control the factors that get us closer to flow and productive creative work more frequently. It means that we can stop relying on inspiration and the hope that maybe today the muse will stop screwing around and finally do her job. It means the whole thing, while still a little unpredictable in terms of which ideas will bubble to the surface, isn't magic.

By far, the hardest work I do as a creator is coming up with ideas, refining them, and seeing where they lead me. I can write for days, but write about what? I have often found myself sitting and staring into the black surface of my coffee, willing an idea to come into my head and hoping in vain for inspiration, before remembering I don't believe in inspiration—at least not in the way it's usually thought of.

I'm in good company in this particular heresy. The painter Chuck Close said, "Inspiration is for amateurs; the rest of us just show up and get to work." Picasso, always a bit contrary, said, "Inspiration exists, but it has to find you working." The poet Charles Baudelaire posited that "Inspiration comes from working."

The myth of inspiration is dangerous because it encourages a wait-and-see attitude. If the best creative minds in the world get their ideas in the shower after late nights with too much alcohol and sleeping in till noon, yet all our slacking off never gets us so much as a funny Instagram caption, where's the hope?

The hope is in doing. It's in recalibrating our understanding of inspiration, which begins with the word itself. Inspiration means to breathe in. When something was an inspired idea, it was something we breathed in from the gods and the muses. We can still rely on breathing in, but these days we have to provide the air ourselves. It's up to us to expose ourselves not only to as much air as possible but the right kind, understanding some air will feed our brains, and some will make us dizzy and giggle suspiciously. Some air is toxic. As a scuba diver, I know there is a lot of attention paid to what's in the air we breathe, which is not just oxygen; in fact, it's only about 21% oxygen, and the rest is mostly nitrogen. Screw with that mix too much without a sense of how to use it and you'll kill yourself.

So it is with creative breathing, if we can call it that. I'm not for a moment suggesting we all need to wildly increase our inputs; I'm suggesting we be much more *intentional* about it. Sometimes the thing we need is not more oxygen in the mix, but a little less.

To abandon the metaphor, what I mean is that it is our job to choose what our brains feed on. Any idea we come up with will be a combination of the other ideas we let in there. The news we watch, the tweets we read, the books, the movies, the podcasts, the conversations with friends—

all of it combines in the brain, incubates over time, and the quality of the ideas we expect to come out relies largely (if not entirely) on the quality of the ideas we allow to enter.

I know it seems I'm harping on social media, but this is one of the reasons I find an unintentional use of it so scary. When we expose ourselves to a great many voices, all of them saying the same things—because so many of us only listen to those with whom we agree, creating the so-called echo chamber effect—we are not exposing ourselves to new ideas. Nor are we necessarily exposing ourselves to good ideas that are well thought out; ideas that *challenge* us and create more than just a knee-jerk response.

But it's not just social media; it's the algorithms. Amazon does this. Order a book, and the site shows you what other people like you are reading. Netflix does this as well, and so does iTunes. And soon *people like us* (whatever that means) are all reading the same books, watching and listening to the same things.

We are becoming more and more homogenous in our inputs, and that isn't helping independent thinking or encouraging individuality. Is it any wonder that our creative output looks less and less individual?

If we want to thrive as creative people, we need to be much more intentional about the inputs. We need to expose ourselves to new ideas from carefully chosen sources. We need to surround ourselves with people who challenge our thinking and not just reinforce our existing thoughts and beliefs. That's one way to find so-called inspiration: to feed the muse.

The other is to put her to work. The muse doesn't do well when she sits still, and because she *is* us, neither do we. I mentioned that my hardest work is often just coming up with ideas. What I learned, and it seems I have to keep re-learning this, is that I don't think in order then to write. I write in order to think.

So if I want ideas, I don't just think. I do. I pull out my biggest Moleskine™ notebook, the one dedicated to ugly scribbles and the generation of bad ideas. It's the one I hope a loved one will burn when I die because the bad ideas outnumber the good ones by a thousand to one. That notebook is full of lists, ideas where I haven't thought much more about the concept than the glimmering of an idea. 10 Ways to Be More Creative. 10 Ways to Make More Money This Month. No matter what comes up, I don't censor myself, I don't edit, and I don't judge. I just write it down.

Making lists is about idea generation, and for me, I need to put pen to paper to do it. And while I may not come up with my best idea ever, it might lead me to a good metaphor. Maybe it leads me to something satirical I could write, like Jonathan Swift's *A Modest Proposal* about eating children so they wouldn't be a burden. Lots of ideas, even the bad ones, are often the very necessary by-product of a process that gets you to the good idea. We shouldn't be afraid of them; we should chase them down and take their milk money.

Of course, ideas are just brain sparks and it's exciting when they happen, but then you've got to see where they lead and that only happens in the real world of putting your hands on the keyboard, the clay, the paintbrushes. You've got to put the muse to work and see where she's taking you. Don't let her off the hook because she's as lazy as we are.

Getting to work isn't the only step toward greater creativity. But it's the one that's hardest to swallow. For many of us, it's easier if we connect that work to a routine or a schedule. I usually write at the same time each day. Some people need the same music (for me, it's Van Morrison). Others need to be in a specific place. What's certainly true is that it's different for all of us.

The idea of getting to work isn't sexy. It's dirt under your fingernails and hands in the soil more than it is head in the clouds. It's paint-splattered blue jeans more than black turtlenecks. It's nuts and bolts more than a bolt from the blue.

The other thing that isn't sexy is admitting our physical world is tightly connected to the creative one. The brain is a physical thing, and while it's not as mysterious as talk of muses and inspiration, I have found that eating well, drinking a lot of water, and getting out of the house once often for a walk or a change of scenery is helpful. I don't do those things naturally, but when I do, my thoughts are clearer and my work is better.

I've found that yoga gets me breathing, and when I return to my work, my brain is firing on cylinders I didn't even know I had. Maybe it's all the oxygen; maybe it's just getting out of my head for a while. But it helps.

It also helps to know your own rhythms. I know some people are super creative in the morning. I work best after or during my first cup of coffee, usually starting around 8 a.m. Some people don't gain momentum until 11 p.m. There's no right way to do it except the way that works for you. I've found my brain shuts off between 1 and 3 p.m. So that's when I do yoga or go for a walk, a bike ride, or a swim. Or I might lie down and read, which is often code for taking a nap. The brain needs sleep, and there's wisdom in getting a good 7–9 hours. And if a nap will make your work better, take one.

The care and feeding of the muse is the care and feeding of yourself and knowing what works best for you. It's in increasing the inputs you expose yourself to, gathering raw materials that challenge you, and taking you out of your comfort zone. It might also be in limiting or changing your inputs. Would we all be less anxious and more focused if we stopped watching the news or checking our phones so neurotically? I think the evolution of technology is vastly outpacing the speed at which our brains can adapt, evolve, rewire, or whatever the right term is. I think we're becoming overwhelmed and unfocused, and the best thing many of us can do is to stop asking our brains to process so much noise so they can get back to focusing on the signal.

The problem with the muse is we're still treating her like a goddess when she's made of more earthly stuff, but that's also the wonder of the muse. Inspiration is ours for the making; it's already there in the paint and the clay and words you're about to put down on paper. How many times have I started to write only to see thoughts come out that I didn't know I knew? How many times has one photograph led to another until I was making work I didn't know I knew how to do? The good stuff is already there, but it only comes out when we begin digging; the shovel is in our hands, not the muse's.

09.
Beautiful Warriors

Like many of us (perhaps even you), I was bullied a lot during my school years. My dad was in the Canadian Army and we moved around a lot, giving me just a few too many first days at new schools, each of them a chance to be the new kid, the one who didn't fit in. The kid with the weird name and target on his back. Don't get me wrong; I gave them plenty of reasons to think I was different, not the least of which was the fact that I made up for my small size with my sarcasm. My mouth had a troubling habit of writing cheques my body couldn't cash.

I remember being on a playground, happily doing what little kids do when they aren't concerned about looking cool, when this larger kid laughed at me, started pushing me around and asking, "How stupid can you get?" Not understanding the concept of the rhetorical question, I said something like, "It looks like you're already pushing the limits." I remember doing a lot of running away as a kid.

Years later, I stopped running. Some older kids at the bus stop started hitting me with a bicycle inner tube that had gone cold and hard in the winter air, and I snapped. I lost it, fighting back through tears freezing to my face, my arms swinging like angry windmills. I got into a fair number of scraps that year. Every day was a fight or felt like one. Forty years later, every day still feels like a (different) fight—one I'm learning to respect, even love, since it shows no signs of going away.

When I first started to play with the idea of a podcast for everyday creative people, I was faced with the need to come up with some visuals for the whole thing, something I could put on the album art and the website. The podcast, like this book, is about creating and making, but I didn't want to use the threadbare images of cameras and paintbrushes because it isn't about the tools we use so much as the perils and rewards of the process itself, and how we live our creative lives.

I don't know exactly how I got there, but I somehow ended up in a little corner of the internet, mesmerized by photographs of Siamese fighting fish, fascinated by the elegant swirling forms and dazzling, impossibly jewel-toned colours. I was intrigued by the fact that, like many creative people, they seem so solitary for most of their lives. But most of all, I was captivated by the Latin name: *betta splendens*, which means *beautiful warrior*. Could there be a more perfect visual metaphor for the daily life of those who struggle to bring things new and authentic into the world, who every morning rise to find that the fears are still there, the work still needs to be done, and none of it comes with any guarantees?

Anyone who has ever had a fight, whether with a bully or the person you love most in this world, knows that a fight is ultimately a struggle of competing ideas. Sometimes one idea or desire wins out over the other; sometimes the skirmish ends in a compromise. In our creative work, we have no shortage of ideas with which to wrestle. Some of them have to do with our inner voices, some with fear or ego, some with the material itself or the medium we work with when it just won't yield to our hands or our will. Other struggles are against external forces telling us to do things the *right* way—*their* way—the way it's *always been done*. We fight the resistance to change; we fight the clock and all the demands of time. Some days we fight the urge just to stay in bed.

One thing seems certain. We must always fight. We must always push forward. And though the fight can be scary, the alternative is worse.

I know it might appear that the writer in the corner who's sipping her coffee and clacking away at the keyboard is just writing, but she's waging battles we'll never see. She's fighting the pressure to be the person her family expects her to be when she hasn't been that person for years. She's fighting the pressure not to write the truth of her life and the knowledge that if she doesn't, she'll implode.

The painter you see putting tentative brush strokes on the blank canvas is fighting for his life, trying to reconcile ideas he's long believed were irreconcilable, and his painting is an exploration or an expression of these new truths, ideas that will seem dangerous or uncomfortable to the people in his world. (An aside: read Chaim Potok's book, *My Name is Asher Lev*.)

That photographer is struggling to find her vision and to find some means of expressing it beyond all the literal work she's made before. She's fighting the suspicion that it's all crap, and the temptation just to go back to what's safe and do more of the same.

Sometimes the fight is so hidden you'd never know, though there she is, there he is—there *you* are—showing up every day to fight, to make forward progress, to tell the truth and get out into the world the stories you've never before had the courage to put into words, or to do something new that might not work. To take a chance. That's a fight. It's not the melodrama of movies with raised voices or easels thrown in rage against the studio walls, paint going everywhere, usually in slow motion. Instead, it's the quiet showing up every day and doing what is hard, and for which we might pay a higher price than we ever imagined just to be fully ourselves and make our art.

A friend recently asked me, "When do I get to live my dreams? When do I get to be the person I want to be, not just the one everyone else expects me to be? When do I get to say the things I need to say, not just what I feel I ought to say?" The all-out effort to be ourselves when every force is pushing us back into a mold that we didn't choose is part of the daily fight.

I was never taught how to fight; my attempts were all fists and rage and flailing around through tears of anger. I was a reluctant and ugly fighter. Until the day my mother enrolled me in judo.

Once I learned to respect the fight, I stopped fearing it so much. The first thing you learn is to bow. Over and over again you acknowledge your opponent, your teacher, even the place where the fight happens. And they bow to you. I wonder what would happen if we all bowed when we walked into the studio, took a deep breath, and acknowledged it. "Today, right now, I'm going to pick a fight." There's something to be said for being in control of that.

Then you learn how to fall down because if there's one thing that's guaranteed, it's that you're going to fall. When I first started my lessons, all we did was learn to fall, over and over again. "This is judo?" I could be falling down at home instead," I thought.

We didn't learn how to avoid falling, but instead how to do it without getting hurt. When I look back at those hours in the dojo, I can still hear the sound of us all repeatedly hitting the mats, our hands slapping the ground to dissipate the energy before we stood up to do it again.

When you fall a thousand times and learn to do it well, you stop fearing the fall. You stop fearing the risk of trying something new or taking on an opponent bigger than you are. And in the absence of that fear, you start to *think* instead. Your head becomes a little clearer; you lean into your training, to all the other moves that you've done hundreds of times, moving into your opponent with a pivot of your hip or the sweep of a leg, each move designed not so much to meet force with force but to take that force and redirect it, combining their energy and yours to throw the opponent to the mat.

Sometimes it's the other way around. You land on the mat so fast you can't think, but you don't need to; you've fallen so many times that it's automatic. And you get up and do it again. The only time I remember getting hurt in judo was when I allowed fear to replace my training and stiffened up as I fell, resisting the flow instead of going with it.

We tend to think that we'd be better off without the fight; I think we're wrong. The fight is what gets us to new places, gives us new skills, helps us see ourselves better, and leads to better art. As Marcus Aurelius wisely stated, "The path of least resistance is a terrible teacher."

Like all my metaphors, this one isn't perfect. But it's helpful to me. Maybe it'll help you, too, just to recognize that it's a daily fight and that the first step to winning it, at least for today, is showing up every day, respecting rather than fearing it, because you see how important it is, that the fight itself is the way of the artist, and that without the fight there is only acquiescing to the status quo and a life without the forward momentum that you alone can direct and steer. Your best art is always on the other side of whatever it is you must fight today.

It helps to know that you've hit the mat many times; though it stings, you're still here, still fighting, bouncing back and learning new lessons, and you'll hit the ground many times more before this is over, and that every single one of those so-called failures can be important lessons and help make you stronger.

Sometimes it just helps to know that your fight is not the only one. You look around the dojo where there are dozens of pairs of fighters, and you realize this is what we're all doing, trying to find our way, and most often, to *make* our way.

One thing is certain: we can't *not* fight. Not if we want to move forward. Not if we want to honour the most pressing voices and desires for our lives. Not if we want to live without the regret of not following our dreams, curiosities, and the what-ifs of which the life creative is made. It's not easy; I know that. For many of us, the struggles to live this life are complicated and painful. But in the absence of any other options, what choice have we but to show up again each morning, bow to that familiar opponent, and throw our hearts and minds into the fray once more? Not so the fight will be over, but so when the next daily match comes, we'll be stronger and more confident in our ability to take a fall and get back up again.

10.
Learning to Drop

Creating anything is an audacious act. It feels wildly presumptuous of us to put ourselves out there into the world while the voice in the back of your head is saying, "I can't do this"! Or "Who am I to do or say this thing? Who wants to hear what I have to say?" Repeatedly in conversations with creative people (and those who could be much more wildly creative), I hear some version of this lament: "I'm just not confident enough." And like so many of the traits we value in the creative process, we seem to believe this is a state of being over which we have no control. We're either born with it or we aren't. I feel like, ever so gently, need to call bullshit on this.

This is a tough one for me. I want to have a conversation about the problem of confidence and the creative spirit, but I'm not sure I'm the guy to have it. I've got ideas about the subject, but who am I to put them out there? See? I can't even talk about confidence without second-guessing myself, which I suppose at least makes me familiar enough with the subject to discuss it experientially. I know what it feels like to lack confidence in myself, my work, and the ideas my work represents.

Like many of you, I live with a tension created by voices in my life, many of them from the past—echoes that seem to have become louder as I've aged rather than disappearing the way an echo is meant to do. I've grown up with conflicting voices—the relentless support of my mother, telling me that I could do just about anything I set my mind to, while my father, a man I saw very little, seemed to be on a critical loop. I still hear him saying, "How could you be so stupid? What were you thinking?" What was I thinking? I was six years old; I was thinking six-year-old thoughts. Aren't they kind of meant to be stupid? Add to this the voices of kids in school, the teachers, total strangers, and eventually, the inevitable critics of whatever it is we make, and it's a wonder any of us have the confidence to sign our own names without second-guessing ourselves.

I want to say we're caught between external voices and the ones that come from the inside, but I'm not sure that's true. When I hear the voice of my dad chastising me as a child, it's not really his voice I hear. It's my own retelling of the story. As I've retold it so many times, along with all the other past and present voices, it has become a different voice—one that comes from a reluctant belief about myself that I reinforce each time I let it run like an uninvited, repetitive script in my head.

And because humans are so prone to confirmation bias, we seize on any evidence that supports our existing beliefs. If we believe that we're not as creative as other people, not as naturally gifted, have fewer talents or whatever other bullshit we've been ruminating on for these many years, we're going to see our initial failures at any activity as confirmation that that belief is well-justified. "See?" we say to ourselves, "I tried it, it didn't work, I'm not good at this." The problem (and it's a big one) is that for any creative effort, we need those failures. We often need many of them.

Creativity is about change; the kind of mutation that happens when we try things that don't quite work but lead us to new solutions that *do* work. And then slowly, one tweak at a time, one new line in the novel or one new change to our technique as a photographer, the results slowly refine. That's how it always works. Unless you give up after the very first failure, convinced yet again that the voices are right.

But which voices are right? For most of us, there are also good voices that have led you to believe that there is a valuable, creative spark in you—the spark that expresses itself as hope or desire. Maybe even a wish, as in, "I wish I were more creative."

It's there; I know it is. You wouldn't be reading this if it weren't. So why is that voice so much quieter, so uncertain? Why is that cautiously held belief so precarious in our hands? I think it's because we fail much more than we succeed in the creative life, and our final successes are so relatively few.

So for every win in the creative life that confirms the

belief that "Yes, I can do this shit; this is what I was born to do!" there are ten chances to reinforce the reluctant but more established belief that we can't. That we're clearly not cut out for this. And over time, the so-called failures stack up, and it feels more and more like those negative voices were right all along: "I can't do this."

I'm not a psychologist. I went to theology school, for God's sake. And I didn't do that very well, either. I bailed on Greek class to learn to juggle, so my approach isn't exactly scientific. But hear me out because everything I just said and everything we believe about ourselves might come down to a juggling lesson.

When I learned to juggle, I was given three balls—two in the left hand, one in the right. I was told to throw one ball from the left in an arc toward the right. Then one from the right to the left. Then one from the left to the right. Each ball thrown before the other lands. Counterintuitively, I was told *not* to catch them. Just let them fall to my feet and do that a while. Throw, throw, throw. And the balls would fall to the ground.

Now, if this is how I had juggled for what eventually became a 12-year career in comedy, you'd be right in thinking I was a pretty lousy juggler. The seasoned performer who can't catch his juggling balls should probably move on to magic tricks. But at the beginning, dropping them wasn't failure. It was *necessary*. I needed to learn the pattern and build some muscle memory. It was baby steps. And once I was really good at the rhythm of throwing and dropping, I tried one round of catching. When viewed really slowly, juggling three balls looks pretty simple and boring, just a repeating pattern of throw, throw, throw, catch, catch, catch. Trust me on this.

During those 12 years, there was only a handful of people to whom I couldn't teach a simple juggling pattern within a few minutes. But the few who couldn't do so were always the ones who paid more attention to the so-called failures than they did to the task of just learning the rhythm and accepting that balls were going to fall all over the place. They were the ones who saw the first balls land on the floor and went immediately to, "See?" I told you I can't do this." And they'd quit. Everyone else understood that dropping was not failure; it was necessary. I told them to do it, and they did.

I think we need to redefine failure. If we can flip the script and see these first efforts not as failure, nor as needing anything that looks like success, then we stop giving our brains the chance to confirm our bias that says we can't do this and to reinforce the voices that say we can. We give ourselves small wins.

To demonstrate, let's go back to juggling. If I were to teach you, the first task would be to throw and drop; dropping is the success. That's the task. And so you did it.

I told you to throw the ball and drop it. Well done. And you thought, "Well, that was easy. I can do this. Look at me throwing and dropping!"

And you did it again and again. When it was time to catch, I took two of the balls away and had you throw one ball from hand to hand again and again. I know very few people who can't do that. "Yeah, but I'm not juggling," you say. Nope. You're not. That is not the task. The task is to throw one ball back and forth. And when you got that down, I gave you a second ball. Throw, throw, catch, catch.

"This is easy!"

Yes, it is.

"I can do this!"

Yup.

And eventually, I gave you three. And you dropped a few, but by then, I'd already given you enough wins that you believed you could do this and displaced the belief that you couldn't. No, you weren't the smoothest juggler. But you could do a round of three. And when that got smooth, you did two rounds, then three, then four, and then you reached for the kerosene and the flaming torches.

The basis of self-confidence is the belief that you can do it, whatever the task is. When we misidentify the task, as in, "I'm going to write a best-selling song," or "I'm going to make a brilliant photograph," we set ourselves up to reinforce our belief that we can't do it, because no one writes the song, makes the masterpiece, or juggles three balls straight out of the gate without a lot of so-called failure. That's not how it works.

But when we identify the task as "I'm going to write the first line of a song and see if it leads anywhere interesting," then all we have to do is sit down and write that one line. And it can be crap. Mission accomplished. You discovered it didn't lead anywhere. But you can do this. So do it again. And again. You'll find that it eventually does lead somewhere because this is how it works. Mutation comes from mistakes and missteps and is never what we expect.

We must redefine failure in the creative life; we must eradicate the notion entirely and replace it with words like exploration, discovery, and experimentation. Words that assume no one specific result. Tell yourself your task is to make a masterpiece, and you will most likely truly fail. But tell yourself your task is to see where your idea leads, to experiment, to write a shitty first draft or a shitty first sentence, and you'll succeed; I don't know anyone who can't write something shitty on their first try.

The creative life is one of failed first efforts. You're meant to drop the ball so you can concentrate on what it feels like to throw it. Catching isn't the point. Not yet. And don't you dare look over your shoulder at the guy who has been juggling for a year. He has a different task than you right now, but he learned the same way you're learning. I know he makes it look easy and you might secretly hate him, but he started just as ugly. And what he's doing now is what you'll be doing in a year. What you don't see is that when no one is looking, he's learning to juggle a five-ball pattern and he's back to throwing and dropping. Throwing and dropping. Over and over. He thinks he'll never be able to juggle five. But that's not his worry right now. His task is throwing and dropping—and he's nailing it.

I'm not suggesting that our struggle with self-confidence is an easy one to overcome. I'm just hoping that with some small realignments, we can make it easier to self-correct, to reinforce the belief, or even just the suspicion, that leads you to think, "I might be able to do this." Of course you can. The creative life is not a rhythm of success leading to success. It's a rhythm of exploration and so-called failures, of necessary missteps and detours, of wild-haired ideas that lead nowhere but to other crazy notions and, every now and then, to something that—to our eternal delight—feels right. Feels like the obvious destination where all those so-called mistakes were leading. Do that a few times, and you'll begin to believe that you're pretty good at making mistakes. But not just making mistakes, because anyone can do that and never create magic. The magic comes in making mistakes and being open to seeing where they lead, not being sidelined by them and believing the lie that we are the sum of our failures and mistakes. We are not. But our work often is, because that's how mutation works.

We've made an unforgiving god of art and creativity, one that demands we neither sin nor fail. But art isn't in the hands of the gods; it's with us. It's made of ashes and dust and the best of it is the best of you—an accumulation of all the efforts and life experiences that make you uniquely *you*.

11.
Where's Your Hall Pass?

When I was a comedian, I started my hour-long stage show by introducing myself and telling my audience, in no uncertain terms, that while I understood their very high expectations for the show, things would go better for all of us if they brought their expectations down to a reasonable level—at which point I'd gesture to a spot somewhere closer to the floor. It was tongue-in-cheek and it got a good laugh, but the principle is a good one.

We judge the success of something relative to our *expectations* of it. Go watch a movie for which you have low expectations and it might surprise you. It might not be amazing, but your reaction is likely to be, "Hey, that wasn't so bad!" But if you go into a movie (like I did with Elton John's *Rocketman*) with high expectations after waiting for six months for its release, only to feel like it was two movies mashed together with sentimental drivel and a cheesy ending, and you're most likely to come out of that experience more disappointed than you might have been had your expectations been lower.

The creative life is full of expectations. If you do any client work at all, you're probably familiar with the idea of expectation management, knowing that keeping the hopes of the client realistic and on track means greater perceived success for the project and a better working relationship.

Expectations—the things we hope for and the outcomes we believe likely in our creative work—can be tremendously dangerous mental artifacts. I'm not sure what else to call them. As a photographer, I've often taught about the way that expectations can blind us to what really is or might be. If you go to a place looking for a specific thing, the intensity of what you're looking or hoping for will blind you to the presence of what is right there, right then.

Expectations are often very specific; they don't tend to be vague. And that's the problem. Their very specificity excludes all the many other possibilities that are out there, and for the creative person trading in divergent ideas and unexpected possibilities, anything that prevents us from seeing those should be held in suspicion.

This is true of the direction of our work; it's true of what we believe about our ability to do that work, and it's true of the reception to our work. The belief that our work will or will not be well-received—the expectation that no one wants to see it and that it's therefore not worth the doing—is not only toxic but sabotaging and self-fulfilling.

It's heartbreaking how often I hear (and always spoken in resignation), "Who wants to hear what I have to say?" Other versions include such hits as "It's all been done; why even try?", "What have I got to offer?" and that timeless ballad, "Who am I to put my stuff out there?" The expected and assumed answers to all of these are, "No one" and "Nothing." And because the expectation's been set, we've answered our own questions already with our assumptions, and we stall right there.

If the last chapter was an attempt to address "Can I do it?", this one is an attempt to answer, "Why should I?"

I'm not alone in thinking that the school systems in which many of us grew up did a great deal of damage to us. Sure, we all know the basics about the world wars, we can place Australia on a map, and you probably know some of the names of the long succession of dead guys who once presided over whichever nation in which you grew up, or at least you did at some point. You might remember what an isosceles triangle is. The contents they tried so hard to beat into my brain are mostly gone now, though I can still draw a wicked cover page for any project I do. That was the part I did best. I always wished there was a class just for cover pages or that every test I did had a cover page requirement. But the *details* are mostly gone. What remains are the deeper lessons. I learned it's important to fit in, to give the right answer, and for anything at all, to ask permission.

Most of us have learned that anything in life requires permission of some kind or another, though as we get older it's less about hall passes to go to the toilet and more about the implied permission we would need to do things our way, to be different, to try some harebrained idea that just kind of arrived out of nowhere and which we cannot shake. If I could reach into your brain and extract all those expectations and replace them with one unlimited, sky blue, carte blanche permission slip, I'd give the world to do that.

You do not need permission. You need no permission to find an answer to the questions I asked earlier in this chapter. Except perhaps from yourself, because if you're asking, "Who wants to hear what I have to say?" it's because you're not out there trying to answer the question. You're asking, but only rhetorically. I hate rhetorical questions, don't you? You already think you know the answer. And you know what? At the beginning, the answer is, well, no one. I know, you thought I was going to tell you the world is just waiting to hear from you. It isn't. Just like before the guy who invented pizzas with the cheese-stuffed crusts, there was no one sitting around thinking, "You know what I want? One of those cheesy-crust pizzas!"

As far as creating metaphors, the cheese-stuffed pizza metaphor marks a new low point for me, but try to stay focused on the point: no one wants to hear from you until you give them a reason. I didn't know I wanted to hear David Bowie until I heard *Absolute Beginners* and had to hear more. I didn't know I wanted to read Hemingway until I read *Farewell to Arms*. I didn't know I liked avocado toast until I tried it. I didn't know I loved my wife and wanted to be with her until she smiled at me.

Who wants your art? No one—until they do. And neither they nor you will ever know that until you make it and share it in some way. I know, it's easy for me to say that. I've already written books. I already have blog readers. Bullshit. We all start somewhere, and the only reason I have blog readers now is because 15 years ago, I started my first blog with none. Not one single reader. And I was asking the same question we all do: who wants to read what I have to say? The difference is, I wasn't asking rhetorically. I was genuinely curious and willing to find out, even if, as I suspected, the answer was no one. David Bowie started at some point with not a single fan. And then he gave those of us who love his music (but before we knew we would) something we loved. Something we resonated with.

In the history of "Which came first, the chicken or the egg?" this one is easy to answer. It's always the artist, never the audience, who comes first. Sure, your audience might be out there, but they don't know it yet. You have to show us. You have to put the work out there in one cataclysmic first act of traumatic self-destruction. It won't be that bad, but it might feel like it.

Here's what you need to know: you are experiencing things as a human being that you alone can convey in the way that you alone can convey. It's true that you are one among billions, but as unique as your story, thoughts, feelings, and questions might be, we all experience similar things. It's the *combination* of those things, and—this is the important part—that you are willing to share them in precisely your own way. That's what will make some of us sit up as your words or art vibrates through every part of us as we see something of our own experience. It's in that moment where we'll suddenly feel less alone and think, "You too?" It is your courage that will give us ours.

Your work will not appeal to everyone; it doesn't need to. It needs to appeal to its own audience, one that the work itself will find as people resonate with it—and see some reflection of themselves in it—and as you give them courage to ask the same questions you do or admit to the same feelings or experiences they've had. You don't have to customize it for them. You don't have to ask, "What does my audience want?" Your art, whatever it is, will find its own audience. Does anyone want to hear what you have to say? They do! But they don't know it until you put it out there and one person finds it and shows it to another and another and another. It has never been so easy for our work to answer that question for us, but we've got to put it out there. Not because it's "good" (whatever that means), but because it's yours.

We gain creative confidence as we take baby steps and give ourselves the chance for our work to answer those haunting questions for us, one at a time. But the expectation that you will launch the blog, the podcast, the new book, or the album to an instant audience, the expectation that only a large audience means your work is worth the making, will stop you in your tracks. Who are you to put your work out there into the world? You're the same one-of-a-kind-yet-just-like-the-rest-of-us person that David Bowie was. Or Hemingway. Or Picasso. Pick whichever artist who haunts your thoughts and reminds you that no, you will never be quite like them, but remember this: they once were a snotty-nosed kid with nothing but rough ideas, picking their way through music lessons, wondering if they'd ever figure that shit out. They wrote crappy first stories, got rejection letters, and at some point, probably wondered, "Who am I to put my stuff out there?" The only difference between them and those of us still in the wings is that they didn't ask that question rhetorically; they answered it with, "Let's find out."

You do not need a hall pass for this life. You need no one's permission to be who you are, to do and say and make what you long for. The fact you were born into this one short, astonishing life, full of possibilities, is your permission. To do it. Say it. Make it. And to do so your way. To let your art *be* the question and the invitation: "Who wants to hear what I have to say?"

But it's more than that. If you're asking the question, there's a good chance that you need to say, make, or do those things for the only audience who really matters—and that's you. When you are stopped by the expectation that no one wants to hear or see or read or listen to what you create, you miss the chance to make that thing, to be surprised by it, to learn from it, to experience the joy and the growth that comes from the making itself. You miss the chance to become the person that art-making always creates. Sure, we make the art, but the art also makes us. In a very real way (without resorting to another dodgy metaphor and to fully exhaust my use of David Bowie as an example), David Bowie became David Bowie by writing his music, singing his songs, slowly mutating, and transforming into the person he became *because of his art-making.*

That's how life works. And that's my way of reminding you that as much as the world needs your art, you need it more. To abandon the making because you're not sure who else might want it is like refusing to cook and eat food because it might not be to someone else's taste. Make your art for you, first. You need it to express yourself, to explore who you are and the story you are living, to sort through the raw materials and become the person that art-making alone can create. You've not only been given permission to do that, but a mandate.

This is a great line from Paul Simon's song, *The Myth of Fingerprint*s:

He says there's no doubt about it
It was the myth of fingerprints
I've seen them all and man
They're all the same

Of course we're all different, but we're also all so much the same. You're not the only one to look for permission to create your work and put it out there. We all wonder who we are to do things our way, to be ourselves, and do our work. But some of us let the question hang in the air, let it call us forward into discovering the many possible and different answers we'll discover as we do the work. It's time to hold those expectations a little more openly, stop assuming we know the answers to these questions, and stop looking for that goddamn hall pass. Who needs what you have to make? You do. You need it more than you will ever know. And we do, too; we just don't know it yet. Please don't rob us of the chance to find out.

12.
Deeper Work

I don't mean to name drop, but I got an email from Seth Godin the other day. Seth is a thought leader in the world of business and marketing, a *New York Times* best-selling author many times over, and I had sent him an email asking about his greatest struggle as a highly productive creative entrepreneur. I was hoping for some generous, pulling-the-veil-back kind of reply, some kind of short quotable wisdom with which to encourage you. What I got, instead, were three words: I am swamped.

That's it? Three words? Had Seth Godin just blown me off? I mean, he's not known for being loquacious, but three words? I don't want to make it sound like he'd know me from Adam, but in a previous email (equally short, now that I think about it), he told me to keep making magic. Seth Godin told *me* to keep making magic! That meant he thought I was already making magic! Was this the start of the bromance I had always hoped for?

But this one felt dismissive. I am swamped? It hurt deep. The bromance was over.

And then I realize he'd given me exactly what I had asked for. It was right there, that was his struggle. He wasn't blowing me off. He was being honest. The other thing I had asked was, "How do you deal with that struggle on a day-to-day basis?" He'd answered that, too. He said no.

Saying no more than you say yes is one of the secrets to being creative and productive. It's not sexy. *Yes* is sexy. Yes is generous. And many of us are yes-ing our way into distraction, exhaustion, and the kind of creative flow that's more like a trickle.

I've talked before about being swamped, and the ways in which we get overwhelmed. In Chapter 03, I compared the flood of requests and distractions (like the email Seth got from me) to a great wave that hovers over us while we tend to all the little things in hopes the boat doesn't fill with water and capsize, which keeps us from getting more important work done. It's a very real threat, and as you do more and more of the work that is truly you and begin to get in the flow and find whatever measure of success you're seeking, it gets worse, not better.

I don't really want to rehash the great wave metaphor or the need to say no. I want to look at the other side of that: the need to say yes to your best work—what Cal Newport calls in his book, *Deep Work*, well, deep work. I like to think of it as core work: the work that is closest to me and supports all the other work I do.

If you're not familiar with Cal Newport, I suggest you look him up. He's an important voice to people like us who create and have work we need to be doing. At first glance, he's also a bit of an unlikely voice to the creative world.

His author photo shows an unsmiling, unassuming guy, someone who's probably good at math and wears chinos. And there's nothing wrong with that; he's just clearly not the "Hey, look at me!" artsy kind of guy. He doesn't look like "the creative type," whatever that means. Nor does his resume. He's a computer science professor at Georgetown University in Washington, D.C.

Creativity is not the exclusive domain of the arts, and in reading Newport, it's clear that he understands people like us. After writing a couple of books specifically for college students about being better college students, he wrote one titled *So Good They Can't Ignore You*, with the provocative subtitle of *Why Following Your Passion is Bad Advice*. I was prepared to hate the book based on the subtitle alone, but I finished it with the conviction that this was a guy worth listening to—a guy who had his hands as much in the real world as in the world of ideas. So when *Deep Work* came out, I bought it the moment I read the subtitle: *Rules for Focused Success in a Distracted World*.

This isn't a book review. But I think the idea that we all have core work, the most important work without which all the other stuff doesn't really matter, is critical. Actually, the idea itself isn't critical so much as our willingness to say yes to that work and do whatever it takes to protect it.

Most of us do not do this well. We create our work in the margins. We do it in whatever time is leftover. Newport argues (and I'm right beside him on this) that we need to carve out blocks of time to do that deep work. Big chunks of undistracted time. I've found this to be true in almost 30 years of day-in and day-out creativity, so I want to offer three ways you might do this without the need to live the life of a hermit: three different blocks of time, some version of which will transform your creative life.

The first is a daily buffer of 30–60 minutes. Get up a little earlier, make your morning coffee, but leave the phone in another room or put it in your bag with the ringer off. Sit somewhere quiet and analogue. Read a poem. Flip through an old journal or write in your current one. Make a list of the next ten projects you'd like to do, or the next three books you want to write, or the next five steps you need to take to get the current work done. This is ideation time, where you fill the need to feed your brain ideas and ruminate on them without other distractions. It's time to wonder, probe deeper questions, and recalibrate the parts of yourself that are probably too busy the rest of the day to hold one coherent thought for very long. This is not the time for calendars and emails and social media. It's time to take stock of the raw materials you'll use in your deep work and to let your muse breathe a little.

The second is a weekly buffer of 3–4 hours, or more if you can pull it off. One block each week when you can *do* what's most meaningful to you. Four hours in the studio to paint, to throw a pot, to get out there with your camera, to *do your work*. The rules are the same as your daily time. No digital distractions, no answering the phone, close the door, keep the kids out; it's just you and the muse. You need to carve out this time. You need it to quiet down, to ramp up the creative flow, and once there, you need a meaningful chunk of time to use that flow and see where it leads. Anyone who regularly experiences that flow knows how fast the time goes. Don't sabotage yourself with one-hour blocks and hope that's enough. It might be. You might be the exception, but I'd bet against it. And if you can do good work in an hour, imagine what you'll be able to do in four. Every week. No exceptions. This is sacred time for you and the muse to get in the ring and hash things out.

The third is a yearly block that's measured in days. Only you can know what's possible for you, but imagine what you might get done in a four-day long weekend away from everyone and everything. Imagine what you'd get done with a week. A "Think Week" has become a necessary part of the creative lives of people like Bill Gates, who twice a year takes one week in seclusion to do undistracted thinking and ideation. Steve Jobs took Think Weeks. So does Mark Zuckerberg.

Seclusion and longer blocks of time aren't a new idea; productive and creative people have been doing this for centuries. The keys are solitude and freedom from distraction. Days to think and work and be free from all the little draws on our attention. Imagine the freedom you could find by going somewhere beyond the signal, to a place where the phone doesn't ping and you're not always one email away from every person who wants a piece of you. For some of you, that's terrifying—but there must be part of you that acknowledges how needful that time is, how good it would feel to be alone with your muse for a while, to do some deep work, to start the novel, to write the songs, to be in the studio for a few days of work and play and nothing else. This time is time to move forward and gain momentum, not just coast on maintaining all the smaller stuff.

Think Weeks aren't a vacation; they're a self-directed week of ideation, recalibration, and getting shit done. For them to work, you probably need some structure. My own times like this allow me eight hours of sleep, and the rest of the time is carved into 2–3-hour blocks. I read a couple of books in some of those blocks, I plan and write lists and brainstorm in some of them, and I sit and write in others. And during the breaks, you could go for a walk, take a swim, or make lunch. Just don't pick up the phone to check in with the world. If you must do that, do it after dinner or the end of the day so it doesn't distract you.

You can do this collaboratively as well. For over 12 years, my manager, Corwin, and I have gotten together for a monthly two-day retreat. Beyond being my manager, Corwin is also my assistant, producer, travel partner, business collaborator, and friend. For years, we've been meeting regularly for this dedicated block of time we call the Think & Drink. At first, the idea was that we'd wander around town for two days, drink beer at different pubs and restaurants, come up with ideas and pitch them to each other, turning those concepts on their heads while making a lot of scribbles in our notebooks between pints.

The drinking has slowed down over the years, replaced by doing. Now we alternate between ideation for a couple of hours, and then put those ideas into action, reworking, rewriting, changing what needs to be changed. These 2–3-day blocks are by far the most productive times over the year. We put them on the calendar and are committed to making them happen. When I was hospitalized nine years ago after shattering both my feet, we kept at it: for months, Corwin would fly four hours to work with me for three days, then go home. We've done it in the remotest parts of Kenya, Italy, the American Southwest, on planes and on boats, in five-star hotels and tents. Almost nothing is allowed to get in the way—it's that productive. When I think about my deep work efforts in business, they follow the same pattern I'm suggesting for other creative deep work: dedicated blocks set aside in small, medium, and larger chunks of time that are zealously protected.

However you do these things (and whether you do them at all) is up to you. What is certain is that all of us can do better and deeper work if we do more than acknowledge that we're swamped and set time aside to do more than just bail the boat to keep us from sinking. Put it on the calendar, move things around, negotiate with your partner, talk to the kids. Telling them Mom needs time to be her best self and do her best work only teaches them to do the same. Having a dad who values his time and his work and models that for the kids isn't taking away from them, it's giving them the gift of a father who is less distracted and firing more often on all cylinders. It teaches the people in our lives that legacy matters to us. That the work of our hands and our hearts is not a frivolous side hustle, but an important part of who we are.

We're all swamped. You're not alone in this. But you alone are the only one who will guard and protect your core work. Seth Godin taking time to answer my email in depth might have gotten me closer to me doing my work, but it wouldn't get him closer to doing his. Seth is responsible for his core work, not mine. I respect Seth now more than ever. And I've been reminded that saying yes to my core work necessarily and often means saying no to the demands of others, as good as they might be. You must protect that core work and the time you need in which to do it.

It's up to you. The world isn't going to give you a break and stop sending emails. Facebook isn't going to let up in its demands on your time—if anything, it'll only ramp up your addiction. It's up to you. It's not going to happen accidentally or spontaneously. Yes, be generous with your time, but know that we all need focused and alone space to do our best work; you've got to create that time and guard it zealously.

13.
Crowdsourcing Joy

Within five minutes on Google this morning, I discovered that you can outsource or crowdsource just about anything. If your relationship has gone south but you don't want to dump your partner yourself, there are people who will do that for you. In Japan, you can outsource people to be friends and pretend to be family. You can outsource or crowdsource the making of reservations, researching a book, choosing a cover for your latest album, and just about any menial task you can imagine. But when, I wonder, did we start outsourcing our joy or crowdsourcing our sense of significance?

My friend Jeffery Saddoris posed a similar question recently when he asked, "Who owns your happiness?" It's a reasonable question, especially among those of us who tie so much of our emotional well-being to the work we create.

It's probably safe to say that most people who engage in everyday creativity (at least those of us not prone to sociopathy or detachment disorders) feel something about our work, often very deeply. And if my observations of friends and colleagues and the famous and now long-dead artists I've met through their biographies are anywhere close to accurate, most of us experience more than our fair share of emotional ups and downs connected to our work.

To be honest, I think it would all be so much *easier* if we didn't care so much. But I don't know anyone who does their creative work with that kind of detachment. We're all too invested, and I think that's a good thing. That investment comes because we pour ourselves into the work. Our work never comes without risk and the need for courage and exploration, often of ourselves. Putting our work out there means we put a piece of ourselves into the world. I think our best work contains more of us than the mediocre stuff that never quite makes it, mostly because the mediocre stuff doesn't have enough of us in it.

Our work and our *selves* are often inseparably entangled. When the work goes well, we're happy. When the work goes poorly, we're not. But I have some questions about this, not the least of which is this: Is happiness the most fulfilling emotional state we could be experiencing in our art-making? Is it the highest thing for which we can reach, or is there something better? And where do we find that better thing? Is it in the feedback? The final product? Or is it in the process itself, in the discovery and the fight to create?

I think these are important questions, not because I think we can avoid the highs and lows that come with the creative life, but because we can make the highs more consistent and predictable, and the paralyzing lows a little less low and a little less frequent. If we can do that and not to level it out completely so that the creative process is placid (a word that's two letters away from flaccid, which is never good), we can enjoy this all a little more and get sidelined a little less. And if we don't enjoy it all the time, we can at very least find something profound and good in it.

When Thomas Jefferson wrote the Declaration of Independence in 1776, he included the right to the pursuit of happiness, among other things: life and liberty. The word "happiness" is an unusually fluffy word for so solemn a document, but it has come to be among our chief pursuits, no matter where you live. "I just want to be happy." But is there something more than happy? And what does happy even mean?

Look it up and you'll find all kinds of definitions for "happy," most of them as fuzzy around the edges as the word itself. Generally, it's about a good feeling derived from positive circumstances. It's the "positive circumstances" part of that definition that makes this problematic. Life has this way of going sideways on us; it's not all rainbows and unicorns. As the Dread Pirate Roberts said to Princess Buttercup in *The Princess Bride*, "Life is pain, Highness. Anyone who says differently is selling something." If we rely on circumstance to bring us happiness, most of the human race will spend our lives living the obverse: unhappiness.

But what if happiness is a smokescreen, a poor counterfeit for something deeper, something arguably harder but much more attainable? What if what we really long for is independent of circumstance and can be experienced, sought, and found, when our work is going well and when it feels like it's going poorly? What if there's something beyond those bright, but relatively rare moments when it's all fireworks and laughter? I think it's not happiness that we're after, but purpose. Meaning. And I think that, in part, because art tells us so.

As I wrote this chapter, I listened to Leonard Cohen's last album, You Want it Darker, over and over on my turntable. On balance, there's very little happy about Cohen's music. It can be dark. Melancholy. Brooding. But it's rich in meaning. And if you spend a day in galleries around the world, you'll find that the art doesn't make us happy. You don't hear a lot of giggling in galleries, at least not from patrons over the age of six and looking at nudes. It's something better. Something more. Art helps us ask better questions, consider deeper things, and find pieces that, when they fit together, begin to give us a sense of who we are. Could it be we're not looking for happiness at all but deeper, more meaningful experiences? Could it be that our art-making is about purpose rather the warm-fuzzies that pop-culture influencers glorify on their well-curated, overly-filtered, social feeds?

Happiness is temporary. It's contingent on other things, almost all of them out of our control. If your happiness depends on other people, then you're crowdsourcing, and the supply will be shallow and unpredictable. But meaning is self-determined. Meaning needs no one to react to the work you make. It needs no likes or comments. It doesn't need the work to go well, though it rejoices when it does, and finds new direction there as much as it does in the failures and missteps. Meaning survives the melancholy and often requires it. Meaning pushes us forward. Sometimes into joy.

It would be wonderful if everything we created made us happy in the same way that it would be great if we could always drink margaritas and eat birthday cake. But it doesn't. And it really wouldn't be. We long for something deeper. We long to make things that have impact. Sometimes, yes, that impact either is, or leads to, happiness. During my career as a comedian, I made thousands and thousands of people laugh, and there's meaning in that, too. But it's not everything. I'm not even sure it's the best thing. Arguably, love is the best thing, and it doesn't always make us happy, either.

I worry that current technologies—more specifically, the way we use these tools—have encouraged us to favour the immediate pleasures of likes and the momentary feeling of dopamine-triggered happiness over a deeper sense of meaning and purpose. I worry that this well-meaning sabotage is getting in the way of people who could be making deeper, more substantially human work. And by that,

I don't mean only the serious, contemplative capital "A" art; we aren't all called to be Leonard Cohen. But we are all called to be human, and to engage with real life and all its complexities. In your writing. In your painting. In your design work. In your coding. There is meaning there. Everyday creativity is profoundly human in activity and scope. It's gritty, soulful stuff. Or it can be. It can make us feel—and even be—more alive. There can be tremendous meaning in that. Meaning that transcends happiness. Meaning that's found in the making itself, as we discover more about ourselves, our work, and the direction it's leading.

The other problem with the pursuit of happiness is the idea of diminishing returns; we're insatiable in our pursuit. We always want more than we have, and so we convince ourselves we'll be happy when we finally wrap our minds around an idea for a project or a book. But to our great surprise, when we get to that point we realize that our happiness lies in *finishing* the book, which proves (yet again) to be a bit of a false summit, the true mountaintop experience awaiting us when the book is *published*, then when it's *well-received*, then a best-seller, then when people stop writing negative Amazon reviews, then when we can turn attention to the next project, and on and on, the carrot of happiness just out of reach. It's great for motivation, as long as you're OK with being miserable and never actually "being happy." But look for meaning, enjoy the work itself, and the years you spend doing it won't feel disappointing the way it feels to chase a carrot you can never have.

Over 2,000 years ago, the writer of the *Bhagavad Gita* suggested we have the right to *do* our work but aren't entitled to *enjoy* the fruits of it—only the work itself. He tells us those who work for results alone will be miserable. I think there's wisdom there, especially among those whose work is creative and so often ends differently than we hoped or expected. If we ask our work not only to carry the burden of becoming what it is but to make us *happy* in the end, we could spend a great deal of our time unhappy. Disappointed. Do that for long, and most of us would just give up.

But if what we look for is more than happy, if we stop relying on the response of others, and on our hopes for the end product itself? If we find meaning in the struggle and the exploration, redefining failure and finding purpose, even joy, in the fight itself, we'll be better off. Because if there's one thing we can count on, it's that most days have some fight in them, even when things are going well. And if it's the journey itself, the fight, the art-making (whatever you want to call it) that you pursue and in which you find meaning and purpose, you're almost guaranteed to find it. Next to that, "happiness" is a consolation prize.

14.
Life at The Improv

In my second year of college, I found myself on my belly flopping around the floor of a small theatre stage, doing my best imitation of sizzling bacon and thinking, "This might just be the best moment of my life." I had joined a comedy troupe, and this was my introduction to improv and a set of rules that I still consider among the most important life lessons I've ever learned—principles that hold an important key to not only being more creative but more comfortably human.

The rules of improv are not complicated and vary depending on who you ask, but there are four universal, guiding principles that keep things on track and keep the actors moving headlong into the funny rather than those long awkward moments that foretell a comic death. That's not to say they guarantee success; no improv actors in the world have been spared the crickets in the audience that signal a wrong turn into the territory of the unfunny. Risk and uncertainty are the stage on which improv plays out, as it is in life. But these rules give the best shot at working well together and moving in a collaborative direction rather than getting derailed, and I don't think it's much of a stretch to see improv as a metaphor for everyday creativity.

The first rule in improv is to agree—to say "yes." You've got to go with things and not fight against them. Saying "no" shuts things down. When I say, "I'm an airplane!" your job is to acknowledge this and move forward with me, not to hijack the scene or try to bend it to your will. Your job is to work with what you've got and see where it leads. The moment you say, "No, you're a turnip," you shut me down and take what little momentum and the spark of an idea I might have had, and you snuff it out or make it very difficult for me to change directions. Off the improv stage, agreeing with *what is* plays out as accepting it and seeing where it leads. It's a willingness to begin in a place of observation and receptivity. Creativity takes place in the very real world of what is and works within our very human limits and constraints. In actuality, the very best of our creativity is a response to what is, not a denial of it. You can fight the universe on this, but it won't change it—not that way. If you do want change, that also begins with acknowledging what is and redirecting the flow.

You do that with the second rule, which is to say, "Yes, *and…*" You've got to contribute. Yes, it's important that you accept the direction already in play, but it's just as important that you add to it, that you bring something different— something distinctly you—to the table and you see where that combination leads. The creative life is not for the passive. You must not wait for permission to engage life and contribute to it, and you won't add a thing to it if you only say yes, if you merely acknowledge things with no desire to question them, improve on them, add to them, or combine them. To do improv well you need to take the wheel now and then and have the courage to steer things in a new direction. It's what makes improv fun: the unexpected and the juxtapositions, the energy that comes from knowing you've just been handed a live grenade, and you've got to think and act quickly.

The third rule is, "make statements." The easy way out of an improv scene is to ask a question. Asking, "You're an airplane? Why are you an airplane?" contributes nothing, and only throws the grenade back into the lap of the other players. It offers no new possibilities, changes no direction, and takes no risks. I'm a big fan of questions. Good questions are the key to an interesting creative life, but you've got to be willing to see where those questions lead, and in improv, that means taking responsibility for choosing a direction and exploring it. That's what creates the tension and the juxtapositions we find so funny. Questions are helpful as they guide us to interesting new possibilities, not as a cop-out or a means of procrastinating. Differently expressed, this third rule could be stated as, "See where the question leads." Take a chance. Run with it. Have fun with it.

Taking a chance is made easier by the fourth rule: There are no mistakes, only opportunities. You don't stop a scene in improv and say, "Wait, cut! This isn't working. I meant to say, 'I'm a dog,' but it came out as, 'I'm a log.' Can we start at the top, please?" I know, it's not the funniest example; don't judge me. But that's improv. Sometimes things just come out of your mouth and it's only that later you think, "Oh, man, if only I'd said this other thing instead." Well, you didn't. You can't unsay it. But you can recognize that by saying it at all, you've created new opportunities and possibilities.

This fourth rule recognizes that often the very best material comes unexpectedly, relinquishing a level of control that surrenders to forward motion. It acknowledges that what is true of improv is true of life: that we're all just making this up as we go. It accepts that dwelling on so-called failures and not seeing accidents, mistakes, or missteps as opportunities is not only unproductive but can carry a heavy cost, one that would require mental and emotional resources that are better spent moving forward rather than looking backward.

We are all making it up as we go; the creative life is improvisation, not a scripted play. It's not an obligatory set of lines and directions written by someone else. But thinking it is can really screw us up. Believing that we've missed our chance, that one misstep or forgotten line can take us out of the game and sideline us. Thinking that one set of decisions might be right and others wrong can be paralyzing. Seeing it as improv and knowing that it's the so-called mistakes that are the funniest and provide the most opportunity to be creative is tremendously liberating. There is no director in improv—no one in the wings we can look to and see if we're doing it right, or doing it well. There is only the sound of the audience, and they are either with you or they aren't. And in those times when they aren't, it's never hard to win them back.

Here are a few other lessons I learned in improv that have helped me navigate the daily creative life. The first is that ego has no place on the stage. You could always tell when someone came on the scene too sure that their way was the right way, determined to get the laughs themselves and not to share them. There was a distinct lack of flexibility, and no matter what you'd say, they would keep trying to shoehorn the scene into their idea instead of the other way around. Nothing is less funny than watching someone try to will the inevitable into a direction it just won't go. Being tremendously creative and productive means letting go, allowing the thing you are making to be more than you, to surpass your initial plans for it—for it to become something all its own.

The creative life does better with humility than with ego. I don't mean you can't be confident. I don't mean you can't believe in your vision and your ability to work toward it; it's just not always about you. At least, not *only* you. Acknowledging that we don't always know where it's going and being willing to hold the steering wheel with a lighter touch often leads to better places and a more fulfilling creative process. You can always tell when an improv actor is more concerned about your opinion of them than about the sketch itself. I think that's true of whatever we make. The more we try to make it about ourselves, the more we get in our own way, and the less it will be about the bigger things the world will respond to and celebrate.

And that brings me to what is arguably the larger lesson in all this, and maybe it's connected to the ego, I don't know. But I do know that the more seriously you take yourself, the less enjoyable improv is, both for you and the audience, and isn't enjoyment (at least in improv) the point of it all? Perhaps it's the point of life, too. The more seriously we take ourselves and the more precious we are about it all, the less willing we will be to take the chance of looking foolish, the fewer risks we take, the more we stay in our comfort zone, the less magic we will experience and create. As Winnie the Pooh so wisely observed, this is too important to take so seriously. The moment you step onto the improv stage, you've got to hold it all with an open hand, see what's going on, and add your own piece to the thing. Without ego or agenda, you've got to take responsibility for your moment on stage and be willing to risk the so-called mistakes, knowing they're the price of entry into the unexpected and the possible. And yes, the audience might laugh at you, but isn't that the point?

15.
Now What?

I've been thinking a lot lately about endings, specifically that feeling that comes when whatever you're working on, or even whichever phase of life you're in, ends. When you get to the end of the pavement on a project and you ship it and you're standing at the edge of the ragged unknown, looking into the vast land in front of you and thinking, "Well, now what?"

I've had more moments like this than I care to admit. I remember feeling it when I knew my comedy career was winding up—when the joy had left and I'd started to feel a new hunger for something more but…what? I've felt it at the end of relationships, and most recently, at the passing of my father; it leaves me with an emptiness that feels like the presence of an absence. And after identifying as a humanitarian and travel photographer for a dozen years, I now feel like the tide is changing again. I'm not sure I want to keep getting on airplanes and spending weeks on end in places that feel less and less like home. But if not that, then what? I have nothing but speculations and suspicions, a collection of maybes and what-ifs. This book is one of them. So is the podcast from which it comes. But after years of coming to this familiar place, this liminal space which isn't quite an end and isn't quite a beginning, I've got some ideas.

Every time I finish a book or a project or launch some new thing, there's this wonderful moment of release, a mixed feeling of relief and joy, and also a bit of loss, knowing that the thing I'd worked so hard on, that has consumed my thoughts and even my affections, as well as my scorn, at times, was gone. Like this constant companion with whom I worked for months or even years has just vanished. There's something quite wonderful about seeing the work of your hands, heart, and mind go out into the world—when it stops being just a possibility in your mind and becomes a tangible thing: an album, a book, a painting, that new thing to which you've signed your name.

If I'm right in saying this feels like a release, I think it's often followed with an anti-climactic sense of being without an anchor, like the boat's been untied from the dock and could just drift forever if you let it. The freedom very quickly gets replaced by something less desirable. I don't know if you can identify with this; this is the problem with you and I being so separated by time and space. If we were sharing a drink or a meal, I could either see your head nodding in agreement or the look in your eyes that says, "This guy needs medication."

But I'm going to gamble that you and I aren't so different. I'm going to assume that you've been there before and asking, "What now?" No matter what you make in your creative life, there is an equivalent of the blank page. It is a daunting thing for something so simple and empty. I think it's the emptiness that makes it so. When it's empty, there is so much possibility, but the moment you put your first mark on it, you declare, "I'm starting here. Of all the places I could begin, I choose to start *here*." And from that moment on, each choice feels like a movement into fewer possibilities, and each move carries with it the risk that it won't be the right move. So we end up sitting there, chewing the end of the pencil and thinking, "What should I do now?" or "Where do I go from here?"

Assuming you'd rather be moving forward than stalled there with your angst and that feeling you get in a dream when you're trying to run but you can't get your legs to move, like you're up to your waist in butterscotch pudding, the answer to those questions is another question: "Where do you want to go?" And if that's not clarifying, how about, "Where is your curiosity leading you?" The standard reply these days seems to be "follow your passion," but I'm beginning to believe that passion is a fuel, not a direction. Passion is a kind of momentum, but it's not a point on the compass. So it's not particularly good advice. It's freeing, but not helpful.

There are better ways to determine your trajectory, and so much of it depends on your personality and the point you're at in your career and life. Circumstance, too. It's amazing how our plans change on a dime. In 2011, I had all kinds of five- and ten-year plans, and then I had an accident in Italy that shattered my feet and it all pivoted so quickly. Suddenly my plans for the coming months and years all got scuttled, and I was lying in a hospital bed thinking, "Now what?" And my questions changed from following my passion to considering my possibilities.

Possibilities are points on a compass. What's truly possible right now is a good start when asking "What next?" because lying there in that bed, my passion—the thing that I most wanted—was to be walking down the street on any corner of any city in the world rather than lying there hoping the nurse wouldn't trip over my catheter tube again. But that wasn't going to happen, not then, so what could I do? I could write. I could write all day long, or as long as the painkillers let me before things got all head-foggy. And during that time, I wrote some of my most heartfelt articles and a book that was mostly coherent. Given the drugs I was on, I call that a win.

But it's not always so clear; our possibilities often seem less obviously constrained by circumstances, and I'd argue that can be a more helpless feeling, creatively speaking, than being stuck in the bed from which I couldn't move. The constraint of being in that bed, the decision made for me, was tremendously freeing in terms of my creativity. So if you're asking, "What are my possibilities?" and the answers are too many to be useful, then consider better questions.

I don't want to tell you which questions to ask, but "Where am I needed most right now?" or "Where can I bring the most value?" might be a good start. "What would I start right now if failure weren't an option?" is another. What's the one thing can't you stop thinking about? What's the one project that scares you the most or demands the most of you? Start steering in that direction.

All of those might be clarifying questions in the sense that they may give you hints about possible next steps. But here's the thing: I suspect it probably doesn't matter where you decide to begin, as much as it matters *that* you begin. That boat I mentioned, the one in which we can feel adrift at times, needs to be moving to steer it. So start anywhere. Put the brush on the canvas, write a first line, put as many irons into the fire as you can and see which one burns brightest and excites you the most. We often cling to this notion that we need to know where we're heading in order to get there, but if we wait until we know where we're heading, many of us will never leave the harbour. Furthermore, it's just not how the creative process works, iterative and evolutionary as it is.

We're so bent out of shape about what the next step is that we forget how speculative this all is. And if you take that step and it leads to a dead-end, better that you get there, find that out, and change course with some speed. But don't get in a flap about it being a mistake; it's just a detour and it could contain the piece you're missing right now to head in the direction that will eventually feel right.

If you're feeling directionless right now, you're not alone. And I don't mean that in an abstract way. I'm right there with you. I'm not exactly drifting—I'm heading somewhere because I'm doing my daily work and sitting down to write. Making my recordings. Making photographs. The boat's in motion, but do I know where? I don't.

I'm at a place of transition right now and asking, "What next?" often enough that it's starting to feel like a mantra. But I'm not asking it helplessly, and I'm not waiting until I have answers before I get moving because it's only in doing the work and exploring the places that work brings me to that I have any daily sense of my progress, and slowly, I see hints of direction—clues to what might be around the corner.

But they are only ever hints. Even when I'm sure I know what's next, even when I think I've got it all figured out. Because we never really know. Asking, "Now what?" is about as honest a question as any artist ever posed, but only if you then go looking, step by step, for the possible replies.

I wonder why we value certainty so highly and act a little embarrassed by the very idea that what we're making right now is just play, just some wild and speculative experiment? When did the creative life become so focused on ideas like mastery that we forgot to engage in the kind of play that alone can lead to that mastery?

So much of this is about perspective and the questions we ask ourselves. Could it be that when we say, "Now what?" or "What next?" it's just not a complete question? Do we mean, "Now what do I do that's a guaranteed success? What do I do now that will take a little less risk and bring the most rewards?" Does that more complete question give you a sense of why you're so paralyzed?

But is that why we create in the first place? To get the most reward for the least work and risk? I don't know why you do what you do, but I've got a feeling it has something to do with the making itself: not because the world needs more photographs, but that *you* need to make them; not because there is a lack of good music, but a lack of *yours*. The magic is in the discovery. That's the reward. If that's the case, the time spent wondering what our next steps might be can be dark and feel lost and drifting.

Here's a segue for you. They say when you feel thirsty, it's already a little late to start drinking water. You should have been drinking all along. The same is true in creativity. Coming to the end of a project and then thinking, "Now what?" with no ideas waiting in the wings is when we risk losing momentum and all the connections that seem to carry over from project to project—those little sparks that die out if we let them.

This is why your notebooks are so important. Some people keep journals and some use programs like Evernote; I use both. I also use my iPhone camera and make photographs and screenshots all the time. Anything I see is fair game. I also use my voice memos when it makes sense to, and I clip together this messy collection of thoughts and what-ifs and questions so that when I finish a project, I have possibilities waiting for me, the signs of which are often already right there in my journal as I become aware of the approaching deadline.

I know it's not romantic to think the muse can't be tamed, but I will work my muse like a rented mule to get my projects done on deadline. I work best that way. A deadline and a production schedule are excellent constraints for me. What the ending looks like is often so different than what I imagined, but the arrival of that ending is never a surprise. Unless it's early, which happens a lot these days as I learn to manage my time better and get more disciplined about doing my work. And if I know when my projects end, I know when the next one begins, and I plan for it.

"Now what?" is an invitation to begin something that is yet unknown with hesitant, speculative, steps. But to do it now. The word is implied by the question. "*Now* what?" Don't put it off. The key isn't the what; it's the now. The what will change by revealing itself to you as you put the first words down, make the first photographs, start the sketches. It doesn't have to be a good start; it just has to be a start.

16.
Second Place

Very few people know that I am an award-winning cartoonist. I wish I could say it's modesty that keeps me from broadcasting that, but the truth is a bit more awkward. When I was in the seventh grade, I had high aspirations of being a professional artist, an ambition that seemed fully endorsed by the universe when my school announced a cartoon-drawing competition. The day the competition was announced, I started my drawing and began writing my acceptance speech. My subject was a music teacher I liked—a large woman named Mrs. Black with notable features and an infectious smile. As I drew her over and over again during the following week, I imagined how flattered she would feel when my caricature of her won the competition. In hindsight, I suppose the things that make a good caricature may not be the things we most want to see lampooned by a 13-year-old. I came to that knowledge the hard way. But this is not about Mrs. Black. This is about the insatiable need to compete and compare.

There's no easy way to put this, so I'll just say it: I won second place in that competition. Certainly not the award I'd been hoping for, but it would have been some consolation had it not been quickly revealed that I was the only kid who had entered. My cartoon was apparently so bad that it lost out to every other person who hadn't bothered to draw one. It was probably that moment that the idea of competition soured for me, and I realized the game was rigged. I don't know who would give a kid second place when he's the only one who showed up for the gig, but I hope they got pink eye. I laugh about it now, but it was deflating to me as the kid who was trying so hard just to be himself and find something he was good at. I guess what I really wanted wasn't just to be good, but to be better-than, and that's always a dangerous aspiration in something as personal as our creative work.

The urge to compete seems to be built into humanity, and if not to compete, then at least to compare. We spend a lot of time looking around. We use other people as our points of reference. Humans seem to find it very difficult, to quote singer and songwriter Bruce Cockburn, "to love ourselves without thinking someone else holds a lower card." It's built-in—a leftover from a time when our place in the tribe was much more a matter of survival than it is now. It's the lizard brain effect, and when the zombie-pocalypse finally comes, I'm sure it'll help some of us survive. But for right now, that competitive or comparative instinct can prevent us from thriving, being ourselves, and making our best work.

American poet e.e. cummings had this to say: "To be nobody but yourself—in a world which is doing its best, night and day, to make you everybody else—means to fight the hardest battle which any human being can fight." Forget the zombies; our hardest battle is to maintain our individuality when the forces around us (and within us) seem hell-bent on pushing us into a mould. And when we look at others to see how well we fit, we're not comparing apples to apples, but something more like apples to elephants; any comparison between the two is meaningless. We know it, but still we persist, comparing our insides to the carefully polished, well-curated outsides of others.

Perhaps we're just looking for clues, searching for signs that show us we're on the right track. But they don't. They only show us where we are in relation to someone else's path. Their progress down that road—and the apparent direction of that road—has nothing to tell us about our own. For all we know, they're backtracking, trying to find their way back to the last place things made sense. Or maybe they're walking in circles. Maybe they're miserable. Their inner journey can't be mapped with external vectors, and neither can ours.

And we know this. So we are told not to compare ourselves to others because the "the only person you should compare yourself to is yourself." It sounds wise, so we nod our heads and think, "Yes, that's very insightful. I'll start doing that instead." Unless you're the kind of guy who wins second place when competing against himself, in which case it's not helpful at all. I think it's also toxic because we don't see ourselves any more objectively than we see others. We see failure and fear and secrets held too tight for too long. We see the ghosts of the past and the hopes of the future, but do many of us really ever see ourselves as we are?

Probably not. Not only is the mirror distorted like those at a carnival funhouse, but perception depends on what we're looking for and on how we see, and I'd argue that most of us are so complex that we're all looking not only at a funhouse mirror but doing so through a kaleidoscope. What we see there is so jumbled that it's no wonder we revert to the simpler comparisons of us vs. them.

So what then? Don't compare. Not with others and not with yourself. Don't look for similarities and don't look for differences. Don't size yourself up and don't allow yourself to feel better or worse based on where you are, where you've been, or where others are or are not. Why must we know which rung of the ladder we stand upon? What good does it do us? More importantly, what harm does it set us up for? If you're me, plenty.

Here's another childhood story. I was riding my bike, though, for reasons that I can only now guess at, I was doing so while looking over my shoulder. Suddenly, I was lying on the ground with a splitting headache looking up at car. I couldn't believe it: I had been hit by a car. But when I stood up and shook it off, the car was parked. No driver in sight, just a big head-shaped dent in the back from the kid who rode his bike into it.

It seems obvious that I shouldn't have been looking over my shoulder. But if I'd been looking at myself in a mirror, I still would have hit the car. In this dodgy metaphor, the former is what happens when we compare ourselves to others; the latter is what happens when we compare ourselves to the image we see of ourselves. Neither should be mistaken for looking forward.

So where do we look? What's "forward" in this analogy? I'm going to suggest that we look to our work and find meaning in that. Yes, learn from others, but keep your eyes on *your* work. Don't worry about what others are doing or thinking. Don't concern yourself about their progress at all. One of the ways to do this is to keep the tension between consumption and creation tilted heavily in favour of making. If you're spending more time on social media or reading or looking at the work of others than you are on your own work, there's a good chance things are pulling in the wrong direction—that you're listening to too many voices and they will drown out the most important one: yours.

This is, of course, why some people spend so much time consuming, because the alternative of mud wrestling the muse and getting our work done can be hard. We call this time looking at what everyone else is doing " inspiration" or " research," but I wonder if it's not often just procrastination, a distraction from the one thing that will be sure to improve our work and get it moving in the right direction: doing our work.

Don't worry about whether you're getting better or doing it right. Don't worry how it measures up, because it doesn't. There is no measure; it's either work you love, work that resonates, work that matters to you, and perhaps, eventually, to others. But it doesn't succeed or fail because it is like or unlike some other thing. You do not become a better artist or craftsman (or however you see yourself) by being more like or different from anyone else. Do your work. Let it challenge you, get it done, trust your gut, and celebrate the small wins.

You're not the only one looking over your shoulder from time to time, hoping to catch a glimpse of yourself in someone else. Or to find some clarity in the differences. But it might help to remember that the goal, at least for most of us, is not to become like another person or do work that is better than theirs, nor is to be different from them. It's not about them at all. It's about you and your work, and as you make your art, it will make you, and get you closer to the person you are becoming. No mould. No template. Just you. That's how it works. Neither art nor life is not about winning; it's about making and becoming, and the meaning we find there. Compared to that, nothing compares.

17.
Hunger > Talent

When Leonard Cohen died on November 07, 2017, the world lost an extraordinary human being: a man of depth and warmth, whose music and poetry were all at once spiritual, political, sensual, and deeply personal. I never got to see Cohen in concert, though his *Live in London* album is about as good as it gets. He's connected with his audience, gracious, generous, and at ease. His golden voice never better, and his presence showing no echoes of his first concert appearance 41 years previous, when he couldn't get his guitar in tune, had to borrow another, and walked off the stage not once but twice before getting through his opening song, finally returning for a third time to finish that song, "Suzanne." There's no way to spin it; he was a wreck. I'm certain if we were in the audience we'd be thinking (like so many people have wrongly thought prematurely about us), "Don't give up your day job, Leonard."

Who we become, and what our creative work becomes, is often so different from how it starts. The beginnings often show no promise at all, but it's often at those beginnings where we judge it the most mercilessly, and from those judgments, decide whether we should or shouldn't continue. So if our initial efforts are such poor evidence, how do we know whether or not to keep going? At what point do we see the writing on the wall and just chuck it all and turn our attention to something else, something we might be better at? And what do we do with the judgments of others and ourselves in evaluating our talent?

I find it interesting that in the world of the arts and creativity, so much praise and attention is given to the rare genius and the prodigy, and, probably more likely, those who *appear* to be so. We look at people for whom every effort comes easily and turns to gold, and we say things like, "I wish I were that talented." But I'd like to see a timeline for every person about whom we say such things. I'd like to see the messy beginnings and the false starts that, in those moments, might have seemed like clear signs of a distinct *lack* of talent.

It is said (though I think we forget it too often) that the absence of evidence is not evidence of absence. In other words, just because the signs don't point to you being brilliant at what you feel called to, especially at the beginning, doesn't mean it's proof you're not. Too often, we look entirely to the wrong evidence. Steve Jobs, Oprah, Bill Gates, and Mark Zuckerberg all dropped out of college. Not exactly promising beginnings or strong evidence for what was to come. Walt Disney was once fired from a Missouri newspaper for "not being creative enough." J.K. Rowling was rejected by 15 publishers before *Harry Potter* found someone to take a chance on it. The classic book *Zen and the Art of Motorcycle Maintenance* was rejected 121 times. I can't even imagine the persistence it took to submit it that 122nd time. Steven King's *Carrie* was rejected 30 times. In his book, *On Writing*, King describes an adolescent version of himself pounding a nail into his bedroom wall on which he began to hang his rejection letters. When the nail gave out from the weight of so many rejections, he replaced it with a spike and kept writing. On the face of it, these so-called failures don't look promising. It would be easy to see them not only as a lack of evidence pointing to talent, but as strong evidence of the lack of it.

It would be hard to argue that any of the people I just mentioned don't have a certain talent for the work they do. But it was clearly never talent alone that got them to where they ended up. Talent is about what we *can* do, but effort is what we do to deploy those talents. Perhaps the largest part of that effort lies in not giving up. Not giving up on the thing we want to do, but also not giving up on the process of discovering what we can do, especially at the beginning when we have no mastery over our tools and we're still exploring the edges of that talent. Early efforts can look like a lack of talent and can be misleading if the dodgy first attempts and the resulting apparent failures put us off the chase.

Talent matters; it's very clear that some people are just better at some things than others. While my math skills are next to non-existent, I do have a proclivity for language and writing and making pictures. I've known it for a long time, but my elementary school teachers would never have seen it. I was a mess. Like Leonard Cohen getting on stage for the first time, you'd never have seen so much as a hint of talent or natural ability back then. It had to be coaxed out.

I wish we were more nuanced about how we define and quantify talent. I think we'd all be so much better off if we talked more about the combination and mix of abilities rather than in binary terms. Talent exists on a spectrum and there are no winners or losers. It's not a you-have-it-or-you-don't kind of thing. Like creativity is not about whether you are or are not creative (we all are), but *how* we are creative differs from one person to the next, so talent is about *how* you are talented, not *whether* you are or not. What combination of abilities and inclinations are part of you, and what do you *do* with that? A mere proclivity isn't the same thing as mastery and refinement and execution. The ability I have to write, for example, will be very different after I've been at it for 60 years than it was when I started at 14. Talent is nothing more than a seed. I have this feeling we all have a combination of those seeds within us, and it's the ones we water and trim and give the most attention to that will one day bear the most fruit.

Seeing talent as a specific thing that you either have or you don't (and which is blindingly obvious from the start) has done more harm than good to otherwise incredibly talented people—the ones whose talent shows up in unlikely combinations and needs unconventional ways of expression and honing. I think that's why school was so harmful to some of us. They just didn't know what to do with the particular mix of abilities and interests that make up our latent talents, no tidy box into which they could put us. And as we felt more and more like we didn't belong in those tidy boxes, we felt more and more like something was wrong with us—that we lacked "talent." Some of us still feel like the square peg in the round hole.

None of us lack talent, though it's abundantly clear that many of us possess it in some unusual combinations. And because no one really knew what to do with that, or how to encourage us in that, we went out on stage, found it scary and awkward, and decided we had no talent for it. And then—unlike Leonard Cohen returning to the stage again and again—we stayed in the wings and decided we'd read the signals wrong, that the hunger and the longing had pointed us in the wrong direction. And we never went out on stage again, robbing ourselves of the only thing that could have eventually made us *really good* at the thing we love, and that's *doing it.*

So what's the difference between those of us who eventually recognize that talent and do something with it and those who don't? For some of us, it was an early voice or influence that saw us for who we were, calling those things forward in us and giving us a place to safely fall down and be awkward while we found our legs. For some, there were voices that actively discouraged those things and eventually blinded us to who we are or might become. For most of us, it's probably a weird mix of both.

The same way some glues attach to one surface better than another, being told as a kid (or even as an adult) that you suck at something is remarkably sticky on our souls and minds, and it stays with us a long time. Mostly because those voices are often right, and the words have a ring of truth to them. At the beginning, many of us do suck at the things we're trying to do. Baby giraffes suck at walking for the first few moments, but man, they get their legs quickly. We get our legs pretty fast when we're uninhibited, especially when it's something for which we have a natural inclination. But it's almost never so fast that someone doesn't see the first efforts and call them out for the awkward thing they are. And because we ourselves have just been thinking we suck at it, we close the box on the talents about to show themselves.

Forget talent and the effort to measure it out, to confirm it or find proof of its absence. What matters is the hunger. That you *want* to do it. That you need to do it. That it brings joy. That you love the chase and the challenge. It'll be some mix of that. What does not matter is the kind of reaction you get at first (or frankly, ever). It's nice if it's positive, but it's mostly irrelevant if not. Early feedback and judgement in either direction can take the fire out of our motivation, and that's what it's about: the fire.

I don't think it matters how good you are or how talented you think you might be. I think it matters how hungry you are. How determined. How willing you are to walk back on stage. How much you love what you do, not how much others love it. Forget talent. Let that be a thing you decide looking back on your life, if at all.

Instead, feed the hunger. Stoke the fire. Something in Leonard Cohen wanted to be a singer, and he kept at it, despite scathing reviews and early evidence to the contrary. It doesn't matter if you don't share my love for Cohen and think, "They were right—he was a terrible singer." Your assessment doesn't matter at all. Not to Cohen. He sang. And those who love him, love him deeply. He had impact and a life in music. And he followed his longing and fed the hunger.

In the 2002 movie, *Adaptation,* Nicolas Cage plays twin screenwriters in what is arguably his only truly remarkable role as an actor. There's a wonderful scene at the end where the twins, Charlie and Donald, are talking. Charlie, being kind of mean to Donald, tells him he was always kind of oblivious. He continues with a story from when Donald was in high school and head over heels in love with Sarah

Marsh, but he never knew she had no interest in him, never knew that this girl made fun of him behind his back. Donald says, "I knew. But I loved Sarah. It was mine, that love. I owned it. Even Sarah didn't have the right to take it away. I can love whoever I want." Charlie says, "But she thought you were pathetic." Donald replies, "That was her business, not mine. You are what you love, not what loves you. That's what I decided a long time ago."

I believe the idea that no one gets to decide what we love is an important one.

Forget the word "talent"; it has come to mean things it doesn't. Talent didn't give Cohen his career on the stage. The seed was there, but what gave him that gift of a life in music was what he did with that talent. It was his perseverance and his willingness to follow the fire in his belly. Not everyone loves Cohen. At times, his reviews were truly bad. But he didn't let others decide what he loved. And he kept at it.

You're not alone in wondering if you've got any real talent or if that talent stacks up against others. You're not alone in wondering if the stage fright is just a sign that you're not cut out for this, whatever *this* is. And you're certainly not the only person who has put your hand to something you want so badly to do, only to find it harder than you thought it would be. You're not the only one to wonder how long it's going to take to get your legs under you.

This isn't just about the big picture, either, but about any of the work you do. Each new project begins the same way and needs time to get over the stage fright and the awkwardness, time to grow, refine, become. Sometimes all we have is that hunger and love.

Talent is a seed. It's a possibility. But it's not a replacement for rigor, and dogged determination. Only the effort makes it shine, shows its promise for what it is. The question isn't, "How talented are you?" but, "How hard are you willing to work to uncover or refine those basic abilities and proclivities? How open are you to the idea that you might not be remotely brilliant at one thing but that being pretty good at a combination of three unlikely things is even better, and that ten years from now you'll have polished that weird combination to a spectacular shine, that even you couldn't have guessed at, never mind the critics blinded by their myopathy?"

I have a feeling that the most wildly creative people you know don't feel especially talented. But they do feel hungry. Feed the hunger. Trust it. Follow the spark. And because it's only in doing what you love for what might be a very long time before it ever becomes the thing you hope for, don't let anyone decide what you get to love.

18.
The Boss of Me

I spent my college years studying theology on the Canadian prairies at two separate colleges both set in the middle of nowhere; locations, one assumes, that were chosen as much for their remoteness as anything else. I suppose when there is literally nothing for miles, it's easier to contemplate eternity and harder to get into the kind of trouble that might imperil young and impressionable souls.

Life at these schools was regulated by sets of rules that now seem draconian to me. Hair had to be a certain length. Dress codes were enforced. Earrings for men were forbidden as well (so I got three of them). We were prohibited from going to cinemas, or, God forbid (literally, apparently), drinking alcohol. Most of all, we had to *think* in certain ways. The church has long frowned darkly on deviance of thought, and though one hopes we're a long way from the days of burning heretics, there have always been repercussions for those who stray from accepted dogma.

It probably comes as no surprise to know that my relationship with the leadership of these schools wasn't always an easy one. My life since then has been one of growing suspicion toward rules, and of rebellion against anyone who tells me what to do. And though I don't go out of my way to drive on the wrong side of the road just to stick it to the man, I will colour wildly outside the lines the moment I have a chance.

Listen carefully to daily conversations and you'll probably find that there are a lot of "shoulds" that get thrown around. A lot of gatekeepers. Obligations. Expectations to act and be and think in certain ways. There are plenty of people who would like to pretend to have the last word, the ones with the word "should" too frequently on their lips and aimed at others. Inexplicably, so many of them are most vocal in the arts and other areas of creativity. But part of being an adult is taking responsibility for our choices and not abdicating those choices to others, though it's a hard switch, isn't it? We spend our childhood years being taught to obey, so when we become adults, we often just keep on acquiescing—trying not to rock the boat.

I wonder whatever happened to that kid who used to put his hands on his hips and yell, "You're not the boss of me!" We were usually wrong at the time; we almost always said that to people who were, in fact, the boss of us, at least for a time. But now that we're truly our own bosses, we've all but forgotten that defiance. And if you're thinking that you *do* actually have a boss, I want to remind you that power is given to others, not taken, and there is no one but you in charge of your life. You are still the boss of you.

Someone told me recently she was a coward, as though that were an inescapable state of being. We are all afraid of something. But fear is not who we are; fear is only a voice. We can listen to it, we can learn from it, we can let it point us in the direction of important (read: scary) work. But we need not obey it. When did we all become so damn obedient? When did we start taking "no" for an answer when we used to be so good at taking the cookie from the cookie jar and pressing the button we were told not to press, just to see what happens? When someone would to insult us, we'd hurl back, "Sticks and stones may break my bones, but words will never hurt me!" It was bullshit, of course. Words hurt more. The scars go much deeper and stay much longer. But at least we were *defiant*.

The art spirit is a lot of things, and one of them is defiant. That word has been rattling around in my brain a lot lately, settling into some old wounds and helping me find new freedoms. It's another way of looking at what I've long called this beautiful anarchy of art-making and creativity. Not because there's value in rebellion for rebellion's sake, but because there is danger in being obedient for the sake of obedience. Conformity pushes the human soul in the wrong direction; it only works because it feels safe. Just keep your head down, blend in, and it'll all be OK. But it never is, not if the cost of being OK is the loss of a fuller expression of who we are. I'd rather be completely me than totally OK. Surely life isn't about keeping the peace and making sure we're not rocking the boat for as long as we can until we slide out of this life without making so much as a ripple?

Innovation, creative thinking, and the making of any new thing is a movement away from what is and what has been done. It's going to encounter resistance. It must. In fact, if it doesn't encounter some resistance from some direction, it's a good sign it's not worth the time. It's going to draw out those who prefer the comfort of what is and what has been over the uncertainty of new and different. And it had damn well better cause some ripples. We need more ripples and less status quo. We need people who are a little less careful with their words and a little more honest. I'm not arguing that we set aside kindness or compassion because we don't need more jerks; I'm arguing that it is a conspicuous lack of compassion to ask ourselves and others to be and do what is not in their hearts where their life and art are concerned, and to spend their lives in service of something they don't have the freedom to question and toward which they have the chance to take a contrary position.

A healthy spirit of defiance has always been part of making art, and though creative efforts have been used just as often to reinforce the status quo, we usually call that propaganda. The Impressionists exhibited defiance in exploring their new techniques and forms. They weren't exactly stuffing rags into bottles filled with fuel and burning cars, but they were defiant. Picasso was defiant in painting *Guer-*

nica. Frida Kahlo was defiant. But for so many of us, these examples feel a world away, so let me suggest another voice against which you, as a creative, need to be defiant: your own inner critic. For some of us, it's not even a single voice as much as it is a choir.

They tell you you *can't*.

They tell you you *shouldn't*, that no one wants what you make so you might as well stop the making.

They tell you you're getting worse, not better.

If it feels like I'm in your head, it's because I hear (or have heard) all of these voices. We all have. And you can either acquiesce or defiantly remind them that they're not the boss of you.

Too many of us are living by rules, expectations, and obligations that we never signed off on. We just kind of eased into them, and when we woke to the reality, we were told just to keep our heads down, don't make a fuss, and everything will be OK. But it's not OK. It is not alright that the things we need to say go unsaid. It's not alright that it's easier to sustain apathy than to care deeply. It's not alright that you have a unique way of seeing this world and, so far as we know, just one life to explore that and hold the mirror up for the rest of us while your own choir of critics is telling you to hold your tongue.

At the risk of sliding into a sermon, you have one short beautiful life, and it's already picking up speed as it heads for the finish line; no matter how many days you're lucky enough to have, they won't be enough since none of us know how many we have until it's too late. There are no prizes handed out at the end for the most cooperative, the ones who risked so little that they got to the end unscathed, but also unknown to themselves and to others because they never took the chance. The only blue ribbon goes to the one who lived fully and on their own terms.

Showing the world (and perhaps especially those we love the most) who we really are is not only a profound act of vulnerability, but of defiance. It's an act of rebellion against the voices that say you're not good enough, that the people you love can handle the lighter parts of you, but not the shadows. To forgive others and yourself and to move on are acts of defiance. So is love. It's an act of all-out anarchy to live and love on your terms and to make whatever it is you make from that place of courage and transparency, to give the world not what it thinks it wants but what it needs, and to take the chance that that gift will be received about as well as the socks your grandmother gave you every Christmas.

In the world of creativity, there are no rules, but there are plenty of voices trying to clamour for our obedience all the same, telling us to sit down and shut up. To play it safe. To just be normal, for God's sake. Bruce Cockburn sang it well: "The trouble with normal is it only gets worse." And if that's where all this rule-following is leading us, then I aim to misbehave, friends. I hope you'll join me.

19.
Too Late to Change?

Sitting with a friend in front of a roaring fire with a glass of whisky, the conversation turned in an unexpected direction when, out of nowhere, he told me he admired how easily I seem to be able to reinvent myself. Others have said this to me before, but it's never stuck like this one did. I was left wondering why my so-called reinventions are worth commenting on at all. After giving it some thought, I think it's a conversation about change and the labels we apply to ourselves that come to define us and make that change difficult, especially as we get older.

If change is the one true constant in life and we're subject to it as much as other things, why does it seem so uncommon and *so hard* to reinvent ourselves? Is it ever too late to evolve or start over, to move in new directions that are unexpected, to others, but often ourselves most of all?

In researching the idea of reinventing ourselves, I kept coming up with articles about artists who got their start "late in life." Musicians who fought and fought and didn't get recognized until (gasp!) their early 30s. Amazing they even let them out of the senior's home. Late in life? Early 30s? Aren't they cute. In your early 30s, you're closer to needing your mother's signature on consent forms than you are to retiring. Then I did a search for "is it too late to change your life?" because I couldn't think of a better search term, and I found myself on a message board where many of the answers were an encouraging, "No! It's never too late! Even if you're in your 30s!" In your 30s? *Please!*

I am fascinated by this question: "Is it too late?" And because so many of us are *not* in our 30s, I wanted to explore the relationship between age and creativity, specifically the idea that because we're a little older, the die has been cast, the concrete has been poured and set, so if you didn't get your handprints into the cement years ago, it's too late now to leave a mark. What rubbish. None of this is really about age; it's about change and the labels we identify with, and those challenges apply no matter how old you are. It's just that we become more aware of the time as we get older. And the labels get harder to peel off.

Is it too late to start over? To change? To do something different, even to be someone different? I think if you are asking the questions at all, it's not too late. But it's like we hit these imaginary milestones and start checking the best-before date like we're a container of dodgy yogurt, and one day past the expiry date we freak out and just want to throw it away. Can yogurt even go bad? Isn't it, by definition, just milk that went bad? Milk shouldn't have a best-before date so much as a yogurt-after date. I like yogurt.

Why are we all so worried that we're going to wake up one day and find that imaginary, only-visible-in-hindsight line and think, "Well, that's it for me"?

Painter Mark Rothko was 43 before he found critical success.

Singer Susan Boyle was 48 when she got noticed on *Britain's Got Talent.*

Helen Downie started painting at age 48, without any formal training, only rose to international fame after a battle with cancer and alcohol (though the fame is not really the point).

Martha Stewart didn't become the Martha Stewart we know until she was almost 50.

Fashion Designer Vera Wang was 41 when she began designing wedding dresses.

The American Folk Artist Anna Mary Robertson Moses, known as Grandma Moses, didn't start painting until she was 78.

Phyllis Diller was 38 when she first tried stand-up comedy.

Colonel Sanders started KFC at 65.

Ronald Reagan entered politics at 55.

Paul Cézanne had his first exhibit when he was 56.

When I was researching this, I found articles addressing the fear that it was too late to start over or find success after 60. I also found articles that said the same things for people after 50, 40, and 30, and even those in their 20s approaching 30 like it was the edge of the known world and beyond which lie dragons.

This is clearly a universal mental obstacle. You're not alone if you feel like you've missed your chance, but you haven't. In fact, I think in many ways, you get more chances as you get older.

You have more experience now than ever. More stories. More wisdom. Why in God's name do we fetishize youth in this culture? I'm not dismissing youth; we need all the inner fire they have. But to discount anyone over 30 because they're not wrinkle-free and they've lost that new car smell is ridiculous. Your taste and sensibilities are more honed. You've lost some of the tolerance for the bullshit and no longer care quite so much about what others think, or if you're not quite there, you've at least learned that others are too busy thinking about themselves to think too critically about what you do. My God, the freedom in having some of that in the rear-view mirror!

I have two beliefs that keep me embracing and pursuing change, which keeps me creatively flexible and willing to move in new directions.

The first is that we don't reinvent ourselves so much as we evolve. To others, it looks like reinvention because we are this one particular person defined by the things we do, and when we suddenly change that, it seems like we've turned on a dime—and aren't we brave? But we don't turn on a dime; the desire for change usually builds slowly in us, the fire growing inside, difficult to see from the outside—but *you* have to see it from the inside. This is, of course, harder than it sounds, because to do that means an admission that change is coming. It's a confrontation between a version of ourselves that we have to be willing to let go of and a version of ourselves that we really don't know yet. Meeting new people is hard, especially when that new person is yourself.

But it doesn't have to be scary. It's still you, and for now, you can entertain the new interest, the new direction, the new admission that "I'm not who I once was" without completely ditching the old labels. A snake grows new skin for a while before shedding the old one; to do otherwise would leave it vulnerable, not unlike the way we feel when we first identify the changes we want to see in our lives and think, "Just how the hell is *that* going to work?"

I think personal evolution becomes harder the more tenaciously we cling to the labels that define us. If I am *only* a photographer, it's going to be hard to wrap my head around the idea that I might wake up one day with no desire to pick up a camera again, and it might be really hard to entertain the growing desire to paint or write poetry instead because "that's not what photographers do." Or if you've been "just a mom" for many years as the kids have grown, you might find it hard to see yourself now as an artist. But does it have to be so binary? Can't you be both for a while, or even forever? Can't you ease in, evolving as a person, recognizing daily change, constantly wondering at the way life and our tastes and desires unfold? Would it harm any of us if the labels we wear were smeared and hard to read?

I've come to see my creativity itself as my path. That's my label, intentionally vague as it is. That path took me into comedy, and it took me out. It took me into photography and design and writing and publishing, and I haven't got the foggiest idea where it might lead me in the future. But because I've been aware enough to see the changes coming and I've let them come without resistance, my so-called re-inventions are just the slow, invisible evolution becoming visible. And because it's slow, I can test the waters before I leap, easing in a little to see how it feels.

Believing that it's our nature to evolve slowly into who we're becoming makes this all so much easier. I also believe it's never too late. The cement never dries. If you're asking the question, if you're longing for change and a new direction, it's never too late. And it's never permanent. If you're a musician who feels pulled away from rock and into jazz, try it out and embrace the zag. If it's for you, you'll find your joy there and discover new directions and challenges. If it's not for you, you can always go back. If you're wondering what other people will think, who cares? They'll think it's interesting; they'll think you're brave for embracing the change; they'll wish they had listened to their gut when change was calling them. With any luck, you'll inspire them to finally do so. But you've got to listen to *your* gut and no one else's.

You might be surrounded by wonderful and supportive people, but that doesn't mean they'll understand. Some of them will misinterpret your change of direction as a loss of sanity or a mid-life crisis. Let them. Some of them will be threatened because they'll now have to experience you through a new filter, and they're wondering how your relationship might change as a result. They're not good with change, either. They might just be worried about you and push you to reconsider. You're allowed to listen to that concern and respectfully decline to change your course. After all, they won't be the one living with the regret of not having followed their dreams. Or maybe they already do, and that's why they're pushing you not to. It's precisely why you need to keep following that desire to change; perhaps it will finally give them the courage to do so themselves.

Creativity is about change. It's about possibilities. And the only time it's too late to change our ideas, our tastes, our creative directions, or even who we believe ourselves to be is when the paint has dried on our lives and we've signed our name to it and called it done. Until then, no one living a life of everyday creativity can escape the need to establish their own relationship to change. It's constant and necessary, and less frightening the more frequently you embrace it. The more you see it as an ally and not an enemy, the more lightly we cling to the labels that others (or we ourselves) use to define us, and the more willing we are to see where new directions lead, the more interesting our creative lives become.

Is it too late to change? To find success (whatever that means to you) in another field of creative endeavour or to explore new ideas and directions? Only you get to decide that. If your answer is yes, then you're right. It probably is. Because it's not your age that determines the answer to this question, but your willingness to follow the muse where she takes you. Very few people succeed solely because they're young, and very few people fail only because they're getting older. We get better as we age, though less nimble. But unless you're wanting to switch gears and become an Olympian or a yoga teacher, it's mental flexibility you need, and that's got nothing to do with age—unless you let it.

20.
Touch the Heart

I woke up this morning under one of those dark clouds that occasionally hover menacingly over people who make a living from their creativity. It's the one from which heavy rains fall in the form of doubts and questions about the ability to sustain our efforts, navigate the next steps, and retire with what we need to avoid spending our last days in a box under a bridge. These are my worst mornings, where even coffee is no consolation, but staying in bed with my thoughts is worse. These are the mornings I wonder why Xanax doesn't come in one of those colourful Pez dispensers. They're the mornings I turn to my old friend Leonard Cohen for the comfort of his words. Today, it was this quote from one of his biographies: "How do we produce work that touches the heart?"

There are two reasons that Cohen's question jarred me from my melancholy and helped me clear the funk that was hanging in the air around me this morning. The first is that it served as a needed distraction. I found myself sitting with my coffee and thinking, "Yeah, Leonard, how do we do that? How do I do that in my writing, or even harder for me, in my photography?" The question set me off in a direction that was considerably more helpful than the others I was asking myself, like whether I'm even employable any more after 25 years as a creative entrepreneur, so I'm grateful for the distraction.

The second reason is that the pursuit of that question (and the work I need to do and explore in order to find anything resembling an answer) is the only way I will continue to be able to keep the other questions at bay—by making, or at least seeking, work that touches the heart.

And I guess there's also a third reason I'm grateful for Cohen's question, and that's that it sent me to write this. Writing and doing and gaining traction will always be more productive and less emotionally exhausting than sitting around worrying.

I don't want to give you the impression that I'm at the edge of a dark hole or that I'm circling the drain: far from it. Right now, I'm in the middle of one of those periods or seasons in life when everything is going really well. My latest book was recently released and is getting enthusiastic reviews, and I'm creating work that's meaningful and, I hope, touches the heart on some level. But it's often in these times when the worry is the worst, when it feels like there's more to lose and further to fall. I've learned to predict these times; they're one of the reasons I keep words from people like Cohen around, to distract me—kind of like you would distract a baby, jangling a set of keys in front of me when it looks like I'm setting up to have a good cry.

Everyone I know has these ups and downs, and when the ups are higher and the downs are lower, the more we care about our work. So on the chance that one of these days is around the corner for you, let's explore the question together: What will it take to produce work that touches the heart?

First, it's important that you know whose heart you want most to connect with. I believe it has to start with yours. As the creator and the maker, it has to begin with you. You have to care. That work needs to be about something you care about in a deeper way than just a passing curiosity. I think there's got to be something at stake. I think if we're doing work that could result in some small failure that we just lightly shrug off, it's not important enough to be doing at all. I'm not saying don't make more of those stock photographs of the ethnically diverse woman in a telephone headset or discouraging you from writing another fluff piece for the Huffington Post. I'm just saying there's probably not much at stake if it doesn't go well, and I doubt you're going to touch hearts. If there's nothing at stake, it's a good sign whatever you make isn't going to touch a nerve. Seth Godin once wrote words to the effect that if it's not worth crying or laughing about, it's probably not worth doing. He was talking about us as the makers of those things, not the consumers, though if it's important enough for us to have those reactions, there's a good chance others might as well.

In order to make the kind of work that makes us laugh or cry, it needs to contain a vulnerability on the part of the maker. Maybe that's the risk in making work that might not go as planned. But it might also be the exploration of some deeper truth or emotion, the honest admission of our fears, our loneliness, doubts, the great love of our life, or whatever other feeling is so wrapped around our hearts that to try to pull it off would just unravel us entirely. The artist willing to put that into their work—to bleed freely and without shame—will make work that strikes a chord and resonates with others who feel the same way but haven't either had the courage to admit it or feel it as deeply as they must to be fully alive.

I think that's what this is all about, really. It's about being fully alive. To do that, we need to be open to deeper themes in our work. There's a reason that the most enduring art has always been the art that doesn't shy away from love and loss, death and sorrow, loneliness, and the brevity of life. The work that endures is the work that comes from people who don't pander or avoid the messier questions and fears. So how do we make work that touches the heart? We make that work about the things that have always unavoidably touched the heart, and we don't turn away from them or smooth out the rough edges that keep snagging our souls.

If you opened the front cover of any of the little black notebooks I've scribbled in over the last few years, you'd find the words of the Persian poet Rumi on the inside cover: "Be a lamp, a lifeboat, a ladder. Help someone's soul heal. Walk out of your house like a shepherd." Not everyone will resonate with these words as an invitation to do their best work, but I sure do. My big question in life with what I do and make is, "Does it matter? Will it be a lamp or a ladder? Will it help someone's soul to heal?" And I ask that question because it keeps me grounded and focused. But pragmatically, it keeps the rain clouds away. It keeps me from worrying neurotically about whether my work is selling or whether my branding is current, or if I should revamp my website or any of the other legitimate but defocusing activities that many of us need to give thought to once in a while. And it does so because next to making work that touches someone's heart, that brings laughter or tears, that gives them freedom where they had none, or gives them an encounter with beauty or makes their life simpler or better, whatever difference you create with what you do, those smaller matters aren't even a drop in the bucket you're hoping to fill.

Whether you make a life or a living (or both) with your craft or art, coding, writing, painting, or whatever it is your hands do at the bidding of your heart, the concerns are always there. I don't know many people who don't worry about the future in some practical way. You aren't alone if you wake up once in a while under the cloud. Please understand I'm not saying there aren't also practical things we can do to make this easier. If your finances or marketing are a mess or if you have other concerns stopping you from making your work at all, all the paradigm shifts in the world aren't going to help.

Whether your concern is art for art's sake (or also leaning on that art to make a living), dwelling on the shadow that is cast by that cloud isn't helping. But chasing work that touches hearts, most especially your own, is its own source of light. And practically speaking, it is the work with the most at stake—the work that contains a vulnerable piece of yourself, that touches courageously on deeper themes, that solves a heartfelt worry or concern for others—that will command higher prices and get more attention because we're drowning in fluffy stuff right now. We're being overwhelmed by the same-old, same-old: stock photographs with no soul that we've seen some version of a hundred times before, products that solve no real human problem except the appetite for more stuff, fiction that offers no hope and explores no deeper struggle, banal art that's as clever as the price is high. But far fewer are the makers and the artists and the everyday creatives who are reaching for a raw nerve within themselves and letting what they make be a response to that—and in so doing, letting it become a lamp, a lifeboat, or a ladder.

It's easy to look into the uncertainty of the creative life and feel helpless. But what if we are the help? What if that's the role of the artists and the innovators? In a world with its share of darkness, flood, and holes from which we're desperate to escape, anyone who makes lamps, lifeboats, or ladders will never lack for an audience or a heart to touch.

21.
Navigating Fog

In Chapter 12, I discussed doing your deep work and being intentional about the time and focus needed to get that work done, and to do it with the kind of depth we all hope will be reflected in our legacy. After I released that same episode on my podcast, I received some emails that reminded me that not everyone knows what this deep work is. Some of the messages were laced with something like despair, and it occurred to me I had never considered the flip side of this coin—the darker and harder side. What do you do when you haven't got direction? When you're nodding your head to all these ideas, but inside your guts are all twisted? When everyone else seems to have this direction and purpose and you just feel like everything is a bit foggy? When you're scared to take a step at all because you don't know where you're going, and that step might take you further from the legacy you're hoping to have or your deeper work?

I wasn't initially sure how to respond to this. I'm still not really sure; how we deal with uncertainty is different for us all. But I have some ideas, most of them a little blurry around the edges themselves because right now, I'm in the soup with you. Right now, I can barely see a hand in front of my face. It feels scary to even admit it, but doing so might be the most honest and helpful thing I can do. We all flounder at some point. We all plateau. We all hit liminal places that aren't really where we used to be and aren't really where we're going—like some dodgy bus stop from which we are eager to escape, but with no idea which bus to take, or when it might come. Hell, some of us aren't sure the bus is ever coming.

When I made a transition from professional comedy to humanitarian photography years ago, it came after a flash of realization on a plane heading to Texas: I didn't want to do comedy anymore. Incredibly, only months later, I was invited to Haiti and I brought my cameras with me. Within an hour of my arrival, everything was clear; I would leave comedy and become a humanitarian photographer. I didn't know how, nor did I know if humanitarian photography was even a thing. I just knew that after years of learning to use my cameras, I finally knew what I wanted to do with those tools. It was crystal clear. Or so the story goes. Looking back, the narrative I've been telling myself feels full of clarity and perfect moments when I'd hit my mark on a map laid out by angels or destiny. But at the time, it was foggy and confusing. Because it did all work out, it's only in the rear-view mirror that it looks like a straight line, but I had no idea where it was leading at the time. Not really. What I did have was the feeling of direction. And even if things were a little unclear, that one point of light was incredibly helpful. At least I could stumble toward it. At least I had direction. When we don't even have that, how do we dare take even one step forward? How would we know what forward is?

Increasingly, the creative people I speak to tell me that points of complete directionless-ness are more and more common. But is this new? As a generation, I wonder if things are really different for us in this sense, or if it's always been this way. I wonder: in the past, in lives that were not under the daily scrutiny of the lens created by social media and the obligation to perform and be the person our branding promises we are, was it easier?

I don't mean to imply that previous generations experienced less floundering, just that they floundered without everyone watching. They'd head out into the fog and thrash around a bit, trying new things, seeking direction by doing and risking, and then quietly coming back to centre before heading off in another direction. And frustrating as that can be, it's probably much easier when no one is looking. I think part of what makes the feeling of directionless-ness so hard is the pressure we feel to *have* that direction. Everyone else looks like they've got it dialled in and that makes us feel like there's something wrong with us.

Today, everyone is looking. That's my most immediate thought when it comes to feeling directionless. While it's ultimately good that there are people out there willing to show the floundering and the false starts in their social media lives, it probably takes an unusually confident person to do so and still meaningfully try new directions. I wonder if part of our feeling of directionless-ness is because the safe places where we used to hammer out that direction (when no one was looking so risks were easier to take and recover from) have largely been taken away from us. Or rather, we've chosen to give them away, throwing the doors wide open to every eye that cares to look in on the part of the process that might better be kept private.

Looking for meaningful direction when none is forthcoming is difficult on a soul-deep level. This is a question about meaning, and because so many people no longer believe in the notion of a divine calling to give them that meaning, we're left to discover it for ourselves. Even those who do believe their calling will come from God usually find God less obvious about things and therefore wind up with the rest of us, having to discover our direction ourselves and being forced to make a choice between too many possible options. This is obviously a deeper conversation that certainly won't be resolved in this book. But I do think that there are some meaningful clues in the fog, small points of light we can walk towards as we look for direction and hints of what our deeper work might be. So where do we find these points of light? By asking three questions.

The first of these questions has been so overused it makes my eyes roll, so let me steal my own thunder and let you know where I'm going with this: we're not looking only for this one answer, but for a common place where the answers to all three questions meet. But forget that for now and answer this question as though it's the only one: What do you love? What makes you come alive and breathe more deeply? What's truly deep-down important and enjoyable to you? Forget the practicalities. Forget what others would think; this isn't their life. In what things do you find your joy? This is a question of the passion that fuels you, but it needs direction, and that's what the other questions are for.

The second question is a bigger one: What does the world need? Not, "What does the world think it needs?" That's too big. What do you think the world needs? Is it environmental conservation? A cure for cancer? Gender equality or shelter for the homeless? Most of us would undoubtedly nod our heads to all of these, but which one really fires you up? Which one gives rise to tears or anger? Which of these would you volunteer for and give your time? Perhaps it's something else. Perhaps you think the world needs solutions to other problems; God knows there are plenty from which to choose. This is a question of mission, and it can be a real clue to our possible direction.

The next question is more personal and demands a certain humility to answer: what are you good at? Forget the false modesty. The question isn't, "What do you do better than anyone anywhere?" It's not a comparison. What are *you* good at? Which combination of things are you good at? Ultimately, you need to get to a point where you know what value you bring to the world, but framed like that, most of us would never come up with an answer, paralyzed by the fear that maybe we don't have value and that the world is too big and we're too small. But in your world—your neighbourhood, circle of friends, your family—what do you bring to the table? Are you the problem-solver, the fixer, the coach, the cheerleader, the one who dries the tears, or the one who makes things beautiful? Figure out what role you play for others and how you make their lives better, and you'll have another clue about possible directions or next steps. You can almost never go wrong walking in a direction where you bring value and make your world, however small, a better place.

What do you love, what does the world need, and what are you good at? The intersection of these three things (and some would add a fourth, what can you get paid for?) is what the Japanese call your *ikigai*: your reason for getting out of bed in the morning and getting to work. For me, this idea of *ikigai* (which roughly translates to "reason for being") is a recalibration tool, a helpful paradigm that keeps me moving in the right direction.

What it does not do is clear the fog entirely. The fog is not a function of my own thinking; it's a function of life. Life is foggy and uncertain. It's been helpful to me to remember that not having the remotest idea of what is coming next or not being able to see the future is not the same as having no direction. You can walk for miles in the fog, and while you might not see what's coming, you can know you're walking in a specific direction.

At the beginning of this chapter, I said I was in the fog with you. I am. But that is not the same as being stalled and directionless. I haven't got a clue as to what's coming next, but I know I'm on the right path. I'm OK with the mystery, as long as I know I'm still on the road. I used a bus-station metaphor earlier, because some of us feel like we're waiting there. But it's not a great metaphor because *there is no bus.* You're it. It's one step in front of the other in this life. And none of us, even the most confident, actually knows what's coming next. None of us know if the deep work we've occupied ourselves with is going to bear fruit or succeed. The novel might flop this time. The album might not come together the way you expected. The product you're working on now that's consuming all your time and focus might in the end just be a faltering step towards something bigger. They are all just momentary landmarks on a journey that'll be clear in hindsight, but rarely is as we move forward into the unknown.

So for those of you feeling like you're navigating in the fog, you're not alone. Creative people live and work in a context of uncertainty. We will *always* be in the fog, and though some days will seem clearer than others, it's always going to be a bit of a gamble. But if you're navigating by the vectors provided by the idea of *ikigai*—the intersection of what you love, what you are good at, and what people need—you'll be walking in the direction of joy and value and contribution, and almost any step you take in that direction will lead somewhere interesting. You'll find work to go all-in on, and projects that quicken your heart and challenge your thinking. And if you've got options and are feeling paralyzed, just pick one.

As long as you're going in the right direction, it probably doesn't matter what you choose. It's more important that you keep moving and not spin your wheels. A tentative step in the right direction, even if it takes you the scenic route, is better than none at all. Moving forward is everything; that's where you find your groove. Whatever you do, don't wait for the bus to come; there is no bus. Don't wait for the fog to clear; it almost never does. The creative life is one of making courageous steps into the unknown, and as long as you're following your curiosity, your talent, and your values, you'll find your way. Embrace the mystery. That's where we experience the joy of discovery and find things bigger than we ever imagined.

22.
It's Not the Tool

When I read *The Revenge of Analog*, by David Sax, it was either an act of subconscious rebellion or plain old irony that I read it on my Kindle. Take that, ye book-loving hipsters. The book itself was a fascinating read, and despite my unprovoked jab at the hipsters, it was one that resonated deeply with me. I read a lot of books, and though I publish digital books, I would much rather read an actual, tangible book. For me, the experience of that is profoundly different than the reading of content on a digital device. I like the smell. I like seeing the cover of the book sitting on my coffee table. I like making notes and dog-earing pages. And anyone who's ever fallen asleep with a book on their face knows that waking up to the cold smack of plastic or glass just isn't the same as waking to the soft caress of paper on skin.

Reading a book-book is just a deeper, more pleasing experience to me than reading a digital one. But all that is really not the point, it's just preamble to assure you, hipster or otherwise, that I have nothing against analog technologies or experiences because in a moment it's going to feel like I've got a bone to pick, and I don't. But there is a movement afoot—both in photography and in our wider culture—that seems to be looking to analog tools as a panacea, or worse, a reason to blame digital technologies for the shortcomings of those things created by it. Suddenly digital is bad and analog is good. What's this got to do with you? I'd like to explore that.

To back up a bit and give you some context for this conversation, it begins in the world of photography, but it doesn't stay there (so if you don't know an f/stop from a bus stop, keep reading). This is all a bit of a reaction to something I read recently, a bit of a rant about what "digital" has done to photography. Among the long list of indictments were charges that digital had opened the door to mediocrity in this once noble craft, that now "everyone was a photographer"—and this was bad. The charges were plentiful: digital lacks soul, is too perfect, has degraded the skills needed to be a photographer in the first place, and has created a culture of homogeny or cookie-cutter mediocrity. Analog, it seems, has none of these problems. Insert eye roll here.

Why I feel the need to respond to any of this at all is not because I feel the slightest need to defend digital technology, but in fact the opposite. I am no apologist for the digital world, nor a critic of analog. I'm most interested in the soul-level matters of the human world, and what I see in the rush to condemn technology for our own failings (or for that matter, to credit it for the moments we manage to shine) is an opportunity for us to find the scapegoat we so often look for when our art or whatever it is we create fails to embody that soul, or skill, or rise above the homogeny and the mediocrity. "Digital" is not some motivated entity responsible for either saving photography or destroying it. It is not the devil. It's just a tool.

Like every technology, "digital" is nothing more than an opportunity; it offers us new ways of doing things. And yes, that new way might include the temptation to do things faster, take less care, or be less mindful. It might open the gates to more people and a lowering of the so-called bar. But it's only ever just an offer. It doesn't force us. In photography, the artist who chooses a digital camera over something made 50 years ago by men with gentle beards and leather aprons is not, by virtue of it being digital, automatically making a choice to walk away from the poetic, the mindful, the importance of craft or the transcendence of mediocrity any more than the artist who chooses a film camera is forced, by virtue of the technology, into poetry, craftsmanship or excellence. To believe otherwise would require us to trust that anything not written on a rusted Underwood typewriter (or better yet, with a quill and ink) is nothing more than modern soulless hackery. I'm not even sure hackery is a word. But I blame my MacBook for that.

It is not art because it's made with film. It's not *not* art because it's made with ones and zeros instead of burning silver on celluloid, which is basically what film photography is. Art is an intensely human activity that will be made with whatever we have at hand. We have painted our art on cave walls using pigments made from berries; we've made it with lasers and paints and computers and yes, quills and ink. It has been made from wood and clay and less noble materials like plastic, glass, and cement. But those are just the means and materials by which we bring that art into the world.

Art is made by us. If you make photographs with soul, it won't be because you used film. If you write screenplays that open eyes or stir hearts, it won't be because you eschewed the laptop and wrote it by hand. If anything you make is deeply authentic, it won't be because the technology itself is authentic, but because you are.

Art is about you, and how you make art is about the way you choose to use your tools. Some people work better with analog tools, some with digital, and some with a mix of these things. Some people prefer the nostalgia that comes with older tools. Or they prefer the way they collaborate with those tools, and when that collaboration is a good fit and feels right, it makes sense that what we create will be better and more fully us. It will feel right in a way that working with other tools won't. The *experience* will be different, which is what *The Revenge of Analog* seemed to be all about. Everyone said film was dead. It's not. They said the same thing about vinyl. As I write this, I'm listening to *Synchronicity* (1983) by the Police on my turntable because I love the experience of vinyl. But I don't think "Every Breath You Take" or "Tea in the Sahara" resonate with me because they're playing on an LP. They're brilliant, resonant songs to begin with.

All of this talk about technology and tools and the idea that analog technologies might be our artistic or creative salvation is because the great temptation with tools or technologies of any kind is the same as the belief in muses: it offers us the chance to blame external influences for our failures. I feel compelled to discuss it because I think that the moment we refuse to abdicate responsibility for what we make, how we make it, and how much of our souls we pour into the making, the sooner we can get back to making art. The sooner we recognize that soul and meaning are found within us and not in the tools we use, the sooner we can get back to attending to those things and seeking them in the places in which they will be found.

But there's another thing, and that's that this knife cuts both ways. There's a snobbery that finds its way into these kinds of discussions (which I can do nothing about), but I can tell those of you who feel that you've been let off the hook and can't make good, meaningful, resonant art because you don't have the latest (or the oldest) and you can't afford the Leica or the RED camera or the new laptop, or whatever tool seems more authentic or that thing that all the pros are using—none of that matters. If you can't make music with the violin in your hands, you won't have the foggiest idea what to do with the Stradivarius. This should give us tremendous freedom and relief. It should place the great joy and opportunity to create and make art back where it belongs: with us. It should free us to use our tools rather than being used by them. It should help us transcend the tools entirely, much as we love and need them.

I think the return to embracing analog technologies is a good thing. It is a recognition that digital technologies on their own are incomplete—that they promised us things they couldn't deliver. It's an acknowledgment that we don't just want high tech; we want high touch. We want things that are uniquely human in our art and creativity that can only come from the human wielding the tool: warmth, soul, the poetry of imperfection, and the ability to touch and feel tools that perhaps have a little more heritage than the plastic and steel thing we hold in our hands, just off the boat from offshore factories. All of these things are good. But don't be fooled into thinking that they offer us hope for a brighter creative future.

That old camera, that thrift store typewriter, or the old acoustic guitar with the dents and the dings didn't come with built-in muses and they aren't a get-out-of-jail-free card. The person who owned it before struggled no less with their creative life than you do. Putting their old tools into your newer hands won't change much for you. And if it does, if it somehow unlocks that thing lurking within you that suddenly frees your creativity and brings your art to life, I promise you, it was there to begin with. Like Dorothy in Oz, we're all looking for the wizard (whether that's some analog tool or the latest and shiniest digital offerings) when it's the ruby slippers we've had all along that will take us home.

I trust you've picked up on the fact that this chapter isn't about whether you use digital or analog technologies, whatever your craft. It's about where we put our creative faith. Time spent blaming our tools is time we are not engaging our imaginations to overcome the limitations of those tools. It's time spent not embracing their intrinsic constraints. The world is full of true believers, some in the promise of digital, some in the hope of analog. Both risk missing what the heretics know and celebrate: that neither offers creative salvation. The art is in you, not the tool.

If you're easily distracted by the promise of those shiny new tools or you've grown weary with them and are hoping to find the magic in some older process, you're not alone. I know I'm painting with some pretty broad brushes; I know that our relationships with our tools, whatever the craft, are not always simple. I want to remind you that *you* are the source of that art, and when our art lacks some *truly vital* thing (like the authenticity that's become such a catchword lately), it won't come from our tools, new or old, and it can't be purchased. When what we make overflows with life and feels right, *that* comes from *us*. We have barriers enough in the creative life; believing that either the credit or the blame for what we make lies in our tools will only shackle us further. What you have is enough, it always has been, because you are enough. And if it's not, if we are not, there is no tool in the world that can help us.

23.
Find What You Love?

I recently returned to the pool in an effort to get my nearly 50-year-old body back into shape after a short absence of only 25 years. I went because I need it, and chose the pool specifically because I love being in the water. I *love* swimming. I love the weightlessness. The rest of it I can do without, specifically swimming around other people which, in even the most modest swim trunks, feels a little closer to public nakedness than I like. Yet I went. And as I cranked out my first modest dozen laps, I kept thinking about the quote by poet Charles Bukowski, "Find what you love and let it kill you." It seemed like good advice for the guy sputtering away, gasping for breath, and wondering what happened to make swimming so damn hard. Maybe it wasn't *good* advice, but it felt like it was going to be prophetic. *Find what you love and let it kill you.* I love swimming, but if Bukowski wasn't dead already (and if I weren't so close to drowning), I'd have pulled my wrinkled ass out of that pool and killed him myself.

"Find what you love and let it kill you" is interesting advice. It sounds so raw and edgy, like something you'd tattoo onto your arm just beneath the one that reads, "It's better to burn out than fade away, man!" But like so many of these existential sound bites, it's a little too short and too shallow to contain the larger truths and deeper wisdom it hints at, and I'm wondering if there isn't a better way.

When I first read that quote from Bukowski, it resonated with me. It felt defiant and made me want to strap on the boxing gloves and listen to "Eye of the Tiger" (the theme song from *Rocky*) on a loop on my iPod. It just rings so loud and true. Even more so when you read it in context. Here's the fuller quote from which the "find what you love" line is so often plucked.

"My dear, find what you love and let it kill you. Let it drain from you your all. Let it cling onto your back and weigh you down into eventual nothingness. Let it kill you, and let it devour your remains. For all things will kill you, both slowly and fastly, but it's much better to be killed by a lover."

What he seems to be saying is that the choices we make in life will ultimately bring about our end, so it's much better, then, to choose things we love. Much better to run out our days doing something we love and giving it our all, letting it preoccupy us and being the thing to which we give our strength. I can get on board with that. What I can no longer get on board with (at least most days) is the exhausting nihilism of this beleaguered and suffering artist who seems to be at the centre of this admonition. Yes, I know art is hard. Life is hard, too. But isn't this all just a little dramatic? Don't get me wrong, I love a good *Dead Poets*

Society-style pep talk, and the concept of *momento mori* (remembering our mortality) is an important one to me. But "better to be killed by a lover"? I don't know.

What about "find what you love and let it give you life and joy and meaning"?

What about "let it make you more alive and not less"?

What about "let it light you on fire and make you a hot, bright burning ember from which others catch heat and light"?

What about, instead, "find the thing that intoxicates you"?

I know I'm all about the metaphors here, but Bukowski isn't the only poet named Charles who's got an admonition for us on how to live well. I like to think that French poet Charles Baudelaire would have looked Charles Bukowski in the eye, raised his glass, and told him to lighten up. In his poem "Enivrez-Vous" (which means "Get Drunk"), Baudelaire's advice was this:

"You have to be always drunk. That's all there is to it—it's the only way. So as not to feel the horrible burden of time that breaks your back and bends you to the earth, you have to be continually drunk.

But on what? Wine, poetry or virtue, as you wish. But be drunk.

And if sometimes, on the steps of a palace or the green grass of a ditch, in the mournful solitude of your room, you wake again, drunkenness already diminishing or gone, ask the wind, the wave, the star, the bird, the clock, everything that is flying, everything that is groaning, everything that is rolling, everything that is singing, everything that is speaking. . .ask what time it is and wind, wave, star, bird, clock will answer you: "It is time to be drunk!

So as not to be the martyred slaves of time, be drunk, be continually drunk! On wine, on poetry or on virtue as you wish."

It would make one hell of a long tattoo, but as far as life advice for the creatives and the artists, I think it serves us better. He's saying celebrate life and be wildly intoxicated with what we've got. Find something to love, whether that's wine, poetry, virtue, or whatever; find something to love and to celebrate and to pursue to the ends of the Earth and let it make you a little head-fogged and heart-twisted. Let it make you alive and give you joy and bring you laughter. Because the alternative of being the "martyred slave of time" is otherwise inevitable. And it doesn't sound like much of a life.

Find what you love and let it consume you like a flame. Let it generate light and turn you into a burning ember. Let it bring warmth and light your days. Let it change you and make you bright. In the end, it doesn't matter what kills you, a lover or otherwise. It matters what gives you life. The dying will happen without much say-so from us. It's more likely that we're taken out by cancer or a drunk driver than by our so-called lover. And then where will we be?

When asked if he wanted to achieve immortality through his art, Woody Allen said no. "I don't want to achieve immortality through my work; I want to achieve immortality through not dying." In other words, sarcastic as he might have been, he was saying living was more important than legacy. Legacy is an idea that I'm exploring more as of late, and it's a hard one for me because I want my work to *matter*. I *want* it to echo into the days beyond which I live. But if most of us are honest, we know it won't. Not for long. Very few people will ever have a legacy that lasts beyond one generation. Fewer still will be remembered 100 years from now. The last thousand years are full of astonishing, famous, notorious people who left legacies that are now forgotten.

Yes, in the short term, legacy matters, if what is meant by "legacy" are the things we teach our children, the way we model a life well-lived, and the way we make the world a better place to those around us: it will ripple out and have more impact than we hope or can ever know. But the longer legacy of books and art and music or any of our creative efforts? I think I'd lose my mind if that was my hope. I can't imagine the pressure.

Did you notice in both poems we are threatened with the backbreaking burden of time and labour? Bukowski admonishes us to find what we love and let it cling to our backs and weigh us down into eventual nothingness.

Baudelaire suggests that we be drunk on what we love as a way to avoid feeling the horrible burden of time that breaks our backs and bends us to the Earth.

Perhaps both of the Charleses are saying a similar thing in different ways and pointing to the same eventualities: that we are all under the dominion of time, that we came from the Earth and will be pressed back into it over the course of our lives. That is inevitable. And it's unlikely that what we do will have the kind of legacy that echoes into eternity, or even the next century.

Bukowski and Baudelaire agree that here and now matters; that we have the agency to choose what gives meaning to the present. They agree that if we don't choose it, now and in every moment, it will be chosen for us. And they agree, it seems, that no matter what we choose, time will keep moving forward with us in its wake until it leaves us shipwrecked on the far shore; that it is far better that we, to the extent that it is in our power to do so, spend that time doing work we love, and that we do it with all our hearts; that we drink our days to the bottom of the glass and enjoy the making and the doing and the moments in between, and slam the glass on the bar for another until the Bartender cuts us off.

This is probably one of the less helpful chapters. I don't see it being particularly actionable. It's really nothing more than Robin Williams climbing onto his desk in *Dead Poets*

Society, chanting "seize the day" and asking his students to do the same.

But poetry has never pretended to be practical. Poetry, like all art, is a call to awaken. It's a call to engage life with eyes and heart wide open, to live in the now, to rise up against whatever is not life. It's a reminder that time is short and ruthless and the greatest thing we can do before we are bent to the Earth completely and the bartender yells "last call" is to be mindful that none of us makes it out alive, that all the things we take so seriously will one day either pass or get the best of us, but in this moment, while we still can, we can choose to get drunk, on wine, perhaps, but also on poetry or painting or spinning clay on the wheel or making photographs or whatever we wish. Yes, art-making is important, and it can be hard. But perhaps when it is hardest, when we are arms-deep in the most important work of our lives, that is the best time to get a little drunk on the love, joy, and delight of what we do and to take chances we might not otherwise risk, and to be a little more generous or vulnerable with our art. To say the things we might not otherwise say in our sobriety. To laugh a little louder than we usually do, to let all our emotions sit a little closer to the surface, and to be just a little messy and more alive.

I don't think we get to choose what kills us, whether we love it or not. But what gives us life is up to each of us every moment of the day.

24.
The Value of Doubt

True believers (and by that, I mean people who never wrestle with doubt) scare me. I've met my share of them in my time, but more hauntingly, I've been one. I'm pleased to say I've grown out of it, but there was a time in my life when what I knew about myself and the world around me was held with much less doubt than it is now. At the time, I prided myself on my conviction, but mostly I was just closed-minded and arrogant. I knew what I knew with a degree of certainty that I don't think we ever have access to as human beings. The world was very black and white for me; not only did I believe the world was held together by absolute truth, I was also unwavering in my belief that I knew that truth absolutely.

My years in theology school as a young adult only helped the cement dry on those beliefs, and by the time I left, they were unshakable and dogmatically inflexible. If you knew me back then and didn't like me very much, I get it. I'm not sure I like that guy either. But he was young, and while he probably wouldn't have much empathy for the man he eventually became, I look back at that young man and all I can think is, "Buckle up, kid. You've got a hell of a ride ahead."

If we're listening, life has a way of revealing the holes in the ideas and beliefs we hold too tightly. During the years I made a living with my comedy magic act, I spent long days studying sleight of hand and illusion, and the only reason any of those magic tricks worked at all was because my audience believed certain things with such conviction that when those convictions were challenged, they would rather believe it was a miracle than believe that they hadn't seen what they were so sure they had. We can be so certain of our assumptions that we become blind to reality. But the problem with assumptions is that we don't see them as such. We believe them to be fact, but not even consciously. Not some tenet of faith that we intentionally adopt, but something silent and unseen, something we don't even know we think or believe.

I bring this up because creative thinking in any discipline, whether it's artistic or not, is about possibility, and it frowns darkly on those who staunchly believe and will not gladly go digging for their assumptions and underlying beliefs to bring them into the light and see if they still ring true. And I don't mean religious beliefs: I mean anything we believe about ourselves; about the work we are doing; about what is possible and what is not; about what we can do, should do, or might do. I'm talking about every assumption about how we believe our work must be done, and why. There is a tremendous value in humility and doubt in the creative life.

It's easy to be convinced. It's easy to rest on things you think you know, learned for good a long time ago. But things change. We discover new things all the time. We once believed with all the certainty of dogma that the sun revolved around the Earth. That the Earth was flat. Or that babies couldn't feel pain. In the early 1920s, we believed radium was good for us. If it could cure cancer, it must be able to cure everything, right? It was put in tonics, hair cream, toothpaste, and even candy. Until it started killing people. And at that point, it was doubt about the safety of radium that led us in the saner direction of, you know, not eating it. Doubt has long been the doorway through which we've walked to innovation and progress: doubt that the old ways are the best ways, that old assumptions and knowledge are the only ways. Doubt leads to questioning, and questioning leads to new ideas and directions.

The problem with doubt is that it really is only a doorway through which we too often peer without walking all the way through to see where it leads. We doubt we can do something, so we don't. We doubt someone's being honest with us, so we disbelieve. We doubt that we're loved, so we act as though we aren't. Doubt used well is not just a lack of belief, but a trigger to exploration. It's a tool, and like all tools, it can be used well, and it can be used destructively—or not at all. Doubt can be used to keep us from our best work, or to push us deeper into exploring that work. If our assumptions are what keep us from seeing new directions and possibilities, it is a healthy, active doubt of those assumptions that will help us through our myopathy, to see beyond what we might be wrong about.

I think the reason we back down from the possibilities that doubt presents us with—the possibility to see things in new ways, to gain new knowledge or ideas, and to try new things—is because not knowing is hard. We've never done well with not knowing. All of the stories of demigods and fairies and demons that we've told ourselves for thousands of years were an attempt to put something meaningful into the empty spaces where we had no knowledge. It's easier for us to tell ourselves stories than to simply say, "I don't know." Especially with things we just *can't* know. It's hard to be the one that stands up and says, "Hang on, that doesn't seem right; are we *sure* about this?" The results of having and giving voice to those kinds of doubts have long been closer to ex-communication, public scorn, and burnings at the stake than they have been to quick changes of heart and mind. We are so, so slow to change our minds. Not just because our pride gets in the way, but because doubting is messy. When we doubt, we stew in cognitive dissonance with competing ideas bouncing around, and what we're left with is mystery.

That, to me, might be the most beautiful aspect of doubt, or the ability to live with it and engage it: the mystery. Where there is no doubt—where there is only certainty—there can be no mystery; without mystery there is no awe. The presence of mystery makes us pay closer attention, to look deeper and longer. It's the flip side of assumption, which isn't so much lazy thinking as it is thinking that has settled into a coma. Without mystery, there is no fascination. Without mystery and doubt, there is no trigger for, "What if?" and it is that question that has long fired the imaginations of creative thinkers and pushed us to look for answers, and in so doing, to find cures for diseases and invent astonishing things and to make and write and perform the best of what we've created. Without "What if?" and "I wonder why?" we'd all still be sitting around a campfire afraid of the dark and the sound of thunder.

Doubt equips us to deal with life because if you're wide awake, it won't be long before you run up against things that don't fit into your worldview. There is so much more out there that we don't know about than what we do. We don't even know ourselves that well. That's why I'd tell my younger self to buckle up and hang on. Because navigating reality without a seatbelt when we're so damn sure of who we are, how we'll react to things, how others will treat us, and what circumstances will throw our way is bound to have its share of collisions. When you believe or know something with 100% certainty and you are then confronted with incontrovertible evidence to the contrary, you can either let doubt do its job and open yourself to the mystery, or you can fight it. Those who fight it turn away from the chance to learn something new about themselves or the world that surrounds them.

The 24-year-old me didn't see life coming the way it did. We never do. He was headstrong and cocksure, closed off to the idea that life and all its mysteries could be anything but what he imagined. That was exactly half a lifetime ago. I've now seen the world from some very dark corners as a humanitarian photographer. I've been twice divorced when I swore I never would—and judged harshly those who had. I've gone bankrupt. I've had more missteps than I ever believed myself capable of. I'm now very sure that my way is not the only way; that my perspective is not the only one. I've become very comfortable with doubt. Life has softened me, particularly in the areas where I once held such rigid beliefs. Doubt has led to possibility: the chance to wonder, to see mystery instead of certainty, to ask, "What if?" and go looking for a response to that infinite question.

It is perhaps ironic, then, that I have never felt more confident. Not the confidence of conviction I once felt (though I'm sure some of that residue remains), but the confidence that it's all leading somewhere. Confidence not that I won't screw up, but that I will bounce back. Confidence that there's much I don't know and the process of discovering those things is better than the certainty they do or don't exist. Confidence that the things I make are necessary, if only to me, and that none of them will last that long, but that's OK. I'm confident that I'm getting a little closer to wisdom. That I'm becoming a more graceful presence in this world and that my thinking is becoming gentler and more accommodating of others. And I'm confident that my doubts are a more faithful teacher than the certainty to which I once clung so tightly. But they will only be so if I let them raise questions for me that I'm willing to explore.

I don't know what your doubts are. I'm guessing many of them need a little more exploring because they're based on assumptions and ideas that just aren't true anymore. That art teacher who told you to give up because you "just weren't creative"? It's time to start doubting her. The parent who told you that you had to have a real job, something more conventional, to be happy or successful? It's time to start doubting that voice. The kids in school, the unhealthy relationships, that one counsellor at summer camp or the professor you had in college—isn't it amazing how the doubts first planted by those voices have become certainties that we've never questioned or assumptions we've never stopped to unravel enough to see for the bullshit they are? It could be they were right. It could be that you're exactly the person those voices tell you that you are:

that you're not good enough, not talented enough. It could be that you're the only one who isn't held back by a little too much certainty, and who couldn't be a little happier, a little more awake to wonder and mystery and the power of asking "what if?" because it can only be asked when we don't already know the answer. It could be you're the only one who wouldn't think more creatively if you saw more possibilities in what you don't know than in what you do.

It could be. But I doubt it.

25.
The Same River Twice

Nothing in British Columbia on Canada's shaggy west coast heralds the coming of spring so unmistakeably as the pink blossoms erupting from the cherry and pear trees. One minute it's winter and the days are short, dark, and wet, then suddenly, winter surrenders to spring, which arrives in a flamboyant explosion of pink and white. The blossoms don't last long—they're here and gone within two weeks of blooming, but they are astonishingly beautiful in those two weeks. Here and then so quickly gone, the cherry blossoms have long been a symbol in Japan of a concept called *mono no aware*, valued not because they have special significance despite their very brief appearance, but for their transience—their exceptionally beautiful impermanence.

As best as I can understand it, *mono no aware* is an empathy toward that impermanence of things, a gentle acceptance and sadness at their temporary-ness. It fascinates me that in Western culture, we seem to have no such equivalent; there is no western tradition of recognizing impermanence, much less celebrating it. It's not that we don't acknowledge that things change, but we seem to react by trying to mitigate and control that change, living in a constant state of denial about it, seeing it as the enemy, and doing what we can to eliminate it. It makes sense then that we, too, have no similar tradition to *wabi-sabi*, the Japanese honouring of decay and imperfection and the natural flow of things.

Twenty-five hundred years ago in Ephesus, a town in what is now modern-day Turkey, there was a Greek philosopher named Heraclitus, and he coined the notion that you can never step into the same river twice. Not only because the water that swirls and eddies around your ankles the first time you wade in that river will be different water the second time around—the first water now long down-river and heading to the sea—but because you are also a different person. Without the modern understanding that most of the cells in our body are replaced roughly every seven to ten years, Heraclitus understood that everything changes; that we and all life are in flux and that the nature of life is change.

Heraclitus is not the only one to observe the impermanence of all things. This fundamental belief shows up in Buddhist thought, as well as Hinduism. And most religions and philosophies have made attempts to define what is eternal or infinite (if anything) and what is not. The latter category is almost always more crowded than the former. But this is not a lesson on the problem of change; it's probably more like a meditation on what we're going to do about it and what the impermanent nature of things means for our creative lives.

If we accept that everything always changes and that we wade daily into new waters as new people—that life isn't as much a matter of *being* who we are than it is about *becoming* who we are—then I think we open ourselves to the idea that creativity itself and all our creative efforts are a tool for exploring and coping with that change. If we step barefoot into that river always acknowledging that these are dark waters into which we've never stepped, then I suspect we do so more awake, more perceptive, and probably more alive, not to mention less neurotic and anxious.

If everything is always changing, then we will find ourselves less presumptuous about what we think we know, less entitled, and less willing to assume that the people in our lives are the same people they used to be. We'll be more open to new needs and desires, both ours and theirs. The assumption, for example, that the person you married 30 years ago still wants the same things (or should) is no less harmful than being blind to your own changes. In other words, however long you remain married, no one stays married to the same person. Recognizing that could keep your relationship moving forward.

In other areas of our lives, the assumption that what worked 20 years ago will or should work now is one of the reasons people experience the so-called mid-life crisis. We fit ourselves into moulds, patterns, and structures at 20 years old that no longer fit the contours of our souls 30 years on. It is not only our waistlines that have changed but the shape of our whole being; the choices we made, the compromises and blind decisions that we squeezed ourselves into when we were practically still kids, may no longer fit. The unhappiest people are those who don't accept the change and find a graceful way to navigate it, clinging instead to what was and who we thought we would always be, blind to the impermanence of everything, including who we are.

This is one reason so many artists experience creative frustration with the creative process. When we find ways of being and working, when we solve a creative problem and figure out what works for us and camp out there once and for all, we repeat ourselves and do work that has no appearance of risk, which is easier, but unsatisfying. And when faced with inevitable changes, we forget that the river flowing around us is already a different river rushing past a changing person, so we panic and try to claw our way back to what once worked for us.

This idea of the Heraclitean river of constant change has made that change easier for me; it allows me to stand in the constant flow of life without my brain exploding and my soul hurting from the kind of bruises we get from trying to resist, to stop it all from moving forward and trying to keep everything the same. I'm trying to find a way to make clear why this perspective changes everything.

As a photographer, one of the more lucid examples lies in the relationship between my craft and my vision—I suspect it's the same for any artist. My vision for what I'm trying to do or say with my photographs is always outpacing my craft or the ability to do and say those things with my available tools and skill because I'm not the artist I was a year ago, and the things I am trying to do or say with my art have changed with me because they *are* me. And as the vision changes, it makes clear the ways in which my craft or technique hasn't kept up—the ways in which that skill is yet unable to express these new ideas. It challenges me and demands that I learn new things and do what I can to bring my skill and my vision to equal levels. But the very act of learning those new skills expands my imagination, gives me new ideas, and propels my vision so that when I wade back into the river, I find it already moving ahead of me, just out of reach. Again. And so it repeats in what would be an exasperating cycle of cause and effect if I refused to see the forward flow of things as not only inevitable but an opportunity for growth. The gulf between what we can imagine and the ways in which we can explore and express our ideas, whatever the craft, can be an engine for our blossoming into the artists we are constantly becoming.

The alternative is decay and stagnation. Those are the two choices. We don't get to choose whether the river keeps flowing or whether we keep changing.; no amount of effort will dam it or divert it. But we do get to choose whether we get into the river and be alive to its motion and flow, or cling desperately to the shore in an attempt to stay at the last point on the river bank when things were working and we felt more certain of our surroundings—even if it was an illusion because the river hasn't been the same for years.

Clinging has never worked. The planet spins too hard and fast. The river moves too quickly. Our desire for things to remain the same, for the cherry blossoms to stay forever, is not only unrealistic but heartbreaking when the blossoms fall, as they always do. The Japanese idea of *mono no aware* frees us to feel sadness at the passing of the blooms, but also joy at the next stage in the life of the tree. It allows us to move forward, ever accepting of the natural rhythm of things. And there's something else, too. When we acknowledge the impermanence of the beautiful things, knowing they will return, we have more freedom to acknowledge the impermanence of harder things and look forward to their passing because we know they will.

Scary as it is, we do not suffer because the river keeps flowing around us, nor that we are also subject to the same changes and flux. We suffer because we cling. We cling to what has been, to what has worked, to things and times and all the ought-to-have-beens and we miss the chance to wade into the changing waters and do what creativity has always done: find a way to become who we are becoming within the flow, and more practically, to solve current problems without getting hung up on the past. And without wearing ourselves out by our efforts to cling to the shore.

I wrote this chapter not because I had answers, but questions. I wonder if so many of our frustrations and hesitations as artists, creatives, or human beings come from the effort to step into the same river twice and the expectation that we'll find it unchanged. Do we make things harder for ourselves, because creativity always happens in uncertainty, when we try to control the flow and direction of that ever-changing, ever-moving river, rather than exploring and even celebrating that impermanence? Does our frustration and paralysis come from trying to cling to the riverbank and resisting that change? And when the change is so clear and calls so relentlessly to us, would it be easier to accept and follow if we acknowledged that we too had changed (or might still) and that all bets were off and all things were, if not possible, then at least not predetermined by what once was? What would you do if you woke up to find you were a different person standing in a different river?

On a deeper level, how much easier would it be to forgive others and ourselves for the past if we acknowledged that everything has changed and that who we were is not who we are or will become? How much easier would it be to take creative risks and try new things if we accepted that our past failures are not a guarantee of more of the same? Nor, for that matter, are past accomplishments a promise that everything we touch will turn to gold. What attachments would you release and how much less devastating would our losses be, if we clung less tightly and saw everything in our lives—and our lives themselves—like the cherry blossoms, more celebrated and anticipated and loved for their impermanence and beauty, not less. How much less might we fear?

The impermanence of all things means one thing above all to me: that now matters. That the person I am at this moment in my life is the one with the opportunity to be fully alive and to use that agency to create, now and not later, and to find joy in that creation and to do so without fear. Where the impermanence of things intersects with my ability to do and to act and to create, there is urgency. Now is when lives are lived; not in the past and not in the future. You will never step into this river twice. Make it count.

26.
Without the Gargoyles

As if people didn't have enough to worry about in the middle ages, churches took to using gargoyles on the top corners of their roofs. Ostensibly to keep the water from running down the stone walls and wrecking the masonry, the long necks of progressively scarier monsters would form a spout and push the water away from the foundation. But the gargoyle itself served a more sinister function. More concerned about the stonework of the churches than about the mental health of their would-be parishioners, these beasts and demons were a reminder to the flock of the terrors that awaited them outside the church, both now and into eternity. I assume the assumption was that anything goes when it comes to securing the salvation of a soul, including fear-mongering. The twin to the gargoyle was the grotesque—similar to the gargoyle though they didn't divert water so they could be placed anywhere you could see them—both serving the dual purpose of keeping God's children in the church and evil spirits out.

Depending on who you ask, the word *gargoyle* came from either the French word for throat, the sound of water going down a drainpipe, or the name of a 6th century dragon that terrorized Rouen and was eventually subdued with a crucifix by the bishop, St. Romanus, before being brought back to Rouen and burned. When the head and neck of the dragon Gargouille refused to surrender to the flames, they did what any reasonable townfolk would do and hung it on the walls of the newly built church. A warning to other dragons and evil spirits and a reminder to all of the dangers of life outside the walls of the church.

Fourteen hundred years later, in a world with fewer dragons, churches have become more subtle in their architectural choices. But the gargoyles remain for many of us, hung from the buttresses of our minds, and some in the very real flesh and blood presence of people we should have chiseled off our building a long time ago. And I'm hoping that by mentioning it, you won't feel like you're the only one who keeps staring up at these reminders of dangers long past that still hang over our heads, threatening us to toe the line and play it safe, acting as if they're keeping you from harm when they're actually keeping you confined and well-controlled.

I don't think I know anyone who still believes in the possibility of an imminent dragon attack. Those in my life who might still worry about these things have been wisely reluctant to bring it up in conversation. But my God, do I know people who are afraid of dangers that are no less able to keep them up at night. And like the original gargoyle, hung from the walls long after the threat had passed, they don't fade away, nor do we look back at them and think, "Thank

God that's over," and move on with our lives. Instead, we see it every time we walk past those walls and are reminded of what we almost lost, what we might lose again, and what exactly we have to fear.

That's how fear works. The head of the dragon mounted somewhere we see it every day doesn't usually relieve our fears but reinforces them. And though the dragon is long dead, he comes back every day and keeps us in line. Remember, we didn't kill it, helpless and running amok like the denizens of Tokyo fleeing before Godzilla; it was St. Romanus. And where's he when we need him?

This is where the metaphor gets pushed beyond the breaking point. Because there are at least three lessons here and I'm not sure which to focus on. The first is that the gargoyles need to be taken down. Not just for the sake of your creative life but probably also *by* your creative life. Many of us are drawn to writing or filmmaking or dance or the like because it offers an escape from the forces that would otherwise keep us down, but we're often unaware that our art or craft also has the power to tear the monsters from the wall and to give us the courage to help others do the same.

But the second implication of this story is that it has to be you; St. Romanus isn't coming. We are all the heroes of our own story, and it must be you who decides to do and make and act in the face of dangers both real and imagined.

The third implication, to jolt us back to the 21st century, is the reminder that it is only a metaphor and the dragon isn't real. That only matters if you believe and act as though that *is* true. When we believe a fiction about ourselves and the world around us, it may not have a grain of truth about it, but believing makes it so, at least to us. Believing the dragons are coming will keep us cowering in our huts and hoping St. Romanus or St. George or whomever else is qualified to vanquish things is on his way.

For many of us, the gargoyles were set on the ramparts years ago: you're not good enough, you're not talented enough, you failed once at something that was hard. Remember that? You and the work of your hands and your heart were dismissed that one time you found the courage to share it with the world. Never again, says the gargoyle. Stay here where it's safe. Beyond these carefully built walls there lie dragons.

Bullshit. Or maybe not. Maybe there really do lie dragons, and they might be scarier than this whole dodgy metaphor. But it remains yours to slay them, silence them, or ignore them. Or prove them liars. And that brings me to the other gargoyles, the ones that in real life surround you with their negativity and their doubts and whose usefulness in your life is probably vastly overrated and their welcome overstayed. So long a part of the architecture of your day-to-day that you can't really imagine life without them, they might even give you some measure of comfort being there. You wouldn't be the first person to become familiar with, or even fall in love with, your captor. And I don't want to make this more dramatic than it is, but how long are you going to put up with the negative people in your life? Those who feign protection when they're the real danger to your spirit, your mind, and the unrealized potential of your ever-shortening life. The ones who promise that life is better within these walls, that it's scary out there, that you *need* them.

They're not St. Romanus, either. You know that, right? It takes an act of extraordinary courage to chisel those people or their influence from your life. That might mean severing ties entirely or finally having a tough conversation and standing up for your needs and desires and drawing some very real lines in the sand. It might mean finally going to see a counsellor because we ourselves are often our own gargoyle, and we need someone to help us see that and shake us free.

All of this matters because safety is a myth that keeps you inside the walls, the doors locked by your fears and comfort, and it's only outside where you live free and able to do your best work uninhibited and liberated from the controls of other voices. It's there you feel the courage and freedom to explore the ideas that define the best of your work, and to find the flow that leads to the work that is most your own. And it could be that before you find that freedom, you need to go find the dragon and pick a fight—and that's scary shit. But it's not as scary as spending your life in dread of it, locked in a dark building with other people who all share the same fear, when what we need most, what we've always needed, was to open the doors wide and let the light in.

I mentioned Godzilla earlier. Have you ever watched those movies? The monster rampages down the street, knocking down buildings and kicking cars aside, while people keep running in front of his marauding feet for blocks on end until they narrowly escape or are squashed under the weight of it all. And as I watch, I'm yelling, "No! Turn down a side street and get behind it! Stop running in the same direction!" And I think that's what I'm doing here with these words, though without the yelling. I'm pleading with you to duck into an alley so you don't have to keep running, so you can catch your breath and do something more helpful and important. Perhaps joining me with whatever you make or do in calling to others to get out of the way and to stop running. You'll probably need to be creative in how you do that. And it won't be easy, or simple. But it will be liberating not to have the fear and the negativity hanging over your head—and to live your life without the gargoyles.

27.
It's What You Do with the Scars

After several surgeries on my feet and a run-in with an axe in the Canadian arctic, my ankles are a mess. One scar, dark and skin-puckered, is referred to in our home irreverently, but not inappropriately, as the cat's asshole. Another is known as Frankenstein, having been opened a couple of times to add, change, and remove some of the hardware in there. That hardware, in x-rays, looks like the junk left over in an Ikea box when you've just built a chair and are pretty sure you're not meant to have six screws, three nuts, and a washer left over, but there it is all the same and you might need it one day, so it joins the others in the a drawer against the inevitable day when you're two screws and a washer short. We call the scar Frankenstein because it's been sewn up so many times the stitch lines just kind of gave up trying to hide themselves.

The third of four scars on my ankles is a big L-shaped line that somehow never got a name. All three of them are the ugly leftovers from a fall I took in Italy nine years ago. The fourth came when an axe glanced off a piece of wood I was chopping, and though it felt like I'd been half-heartedly hit with a baseball bat, the axe cut through my pant, my boot, and deep into my ankle. Not ideal at any time, this particular incident set us to striking camp around midnight and heading down the Yukon's forbidding Dempster Highway dodging potholes that could swallow a moose, while keeping an eye open for those same moose. We drove into Dawson City, which, despite its name, is barely a town and has no hospital. It does have a nurse if you can find her, which we did after going to the police station which was very dark and very closed, but had a phone on the wall outside to call the next largest town, Whitehorse (over an hour away), in hopes they might send someone. They eventually did just that, and I was stitched up at three o'clock in the morning.

Like I said, my ankles are a mess. But there are other scars, too. I've got a crescent moon on my right thumb, put there with a Swiss Army knife when I was about 8 years old on a camping trip in Nova Scotia. I've got a similar-shaped scar above one of my eyes (though I can never remember which one because when I look in the mirror left becomes right and vice versa and apparently, it's easier to go look in the mirror than to remember these things). I got that one when I was roped into being a referee at a hockey game and had to borrow a pair of skates that hadn't been sharpened since the game was invented. At the opening face-off, I dropped the puck and, to the amazement of the crowd, then did a complete front flip as my skates shot out from under me and I cunningly stopped my forward momentum with my face.

That permanent mark now keeps company with the others: three small scars that testify to my gallbladder's departure, one from a hernia repair, and a small assortment on my knees from learning to ride a bike. Oddly, there are a couple that I look at and, for the life of me, I can't remember where they came from.

This inventory of scars is a little like an evidence locker in one of those cops shows, though they testify to different things. Some of them are incontrovertible proof of my own stupidity. Some are a witness to my inability to grasp basic physics or the law of gravity. And some to the fact that my body, too, is subject to the same kind of wear and tear as the rest of creation.

Those are the scars you can see. There are many more under the surface, in my heart and mind—I'm betting you've got a few yourself. The scars I carry on the inside, the emotional ones wrapped in memories, don't hurt the way my ankles do when it gets cold and wet out; it's a different kind of hurt, and they ache at the strangest times. When I'm least expecting it, they remind me of mistakes and losses, failures and betrayals, both those I've suffered and those I have caused. I can tell the difference because most of the time it's the pangs from the latter that hurt more.

One of the advantages of getting older is that the pain from the external scars mostly fades. There are still a couple where I've lost some of the sensation and they feel strange when I touch them, but mostly, they're like the creases in once-bent-over pages in any of the books on my shelf; they're the dog-ears and chapter markers of a well-loved story that was too large to read in one sitting. At least the ones you can see. The ones on the inside remain sensitive for longer, but they aren't the bent pages; they're a bigger part of the story. They're a reminder of the twists and turns of the plot and the shitty things authors sometimes do to their characters or allow their characters to do to themselves and others. We're all in our own story and the best stories have always depended on some pretty hard moments. They're nasty things to live through, but they make us who we are. I suppose it's better than living a story no one wants to read—a story with nothing to risk but also nothing to gain, though that's small comfort at the time.

I have never been ashamed of my scars. Perhaps I always bought the line that "chicks dig scars." I see that jagged zippered line across my foot and I hear Indiana Jones telling Marion, " It's not the years, honey. It's the mileage." The scars don't only testify to my missteps but to my resilience and to lessons learned. When I was a kid, I had occasion to write lines on the board: I will not run in the halls, I will not run in the halls, I will not run in the halls. Write that a hundred times and you might begin to slow down in the halls, though probably not for long. But these scars are lines written in flesh and most of them only needed writing once. They are reminders of some of the more interesting, if not also painful, lessons and detours in my life, hints to some of the greatest victories, and they are now the source of the best I have to offer as a writer and a human being, most especially the scars on the inside.

These dents and scratches are not something I regret, at least not now that I've lived with them a while and the pain that created them has faded. They remind me that what doesn't kill us only gives us something to blog about; that the last thing I need to worry about when it comes to this body is resale value at the end. They remind me that I am not the good china, only to be used on special occasions. They remind me that things that are well-loved are well used, and probably show it.

I don't *want* to get to the end in pristine condition, but rather well-loved and full of stories, and to do that, there's a good chance some of the parts will be hanging by a thread toward the end, which I very much hope is a long way off.

When we stop seeing our scars—whatever they are—as a thing that was done *to* us, a reminder only of the pain and the past and an unfixable scratch on the paint that lowers the value or makes us unsightly, unlovable, or unusable, and begin to see them instead as qualifications and patina and evidence of a life well-lived and well-learned, we might begin to dip into the great wealth of those experiences and find in them the raw materials for our art.

I once read a great line from writer Madeleine L'Engle that said something brilliant to the effect that as we go through life, we all suffer injuries, but that the most grievous harm, far greater than the original hurt, is caused by how we react to them. She was pointing to the tendency to hide our scars, to build walls around the more tender parts, to become self-protective and ashamed, and to retreat away from risk—and in doing so, we begin to shrivel, to become numb, and to atrophy. That is the true damage.

I don't know if you have to suffer to be an artist. I suspect that's partly true, but that's not exactly setting the bar very high, is it? I mean, *everyone* suffers. No one is immune from the bumps and bruises of life. Some of us encounter far more pain and loss than we ever thought we could bear. Some people live enough hard stories to fill a library. I don't want to romanticize pain and suffering or imply that there's some golden nugget in all of it that makes it easier to bear. But I think it's important we acknowledge it, to be unflinching in our acceptance of it as having happened—as *always* happening—both to ourselves and others, and to look it in the eye and refuse to allow it to kill our spirits.

And if art is on your mind, if making something larger than your pain and bigger than your scars matters to you, then it doesn't matter whether you have to suffer as an artist. It matters whether you're willing to share it, to use it, and to roll up your sleeves and show your scars rather than hide them. Because somewhere out there are other timid souls freshly wounded and wondering if they'll make it through, wondering if this won't just kill them dead on the spot, and they don't have the benefit of hindsight; right in the middle of their doubt and fear, they can't look at the scars that'll one day form around this present hurt and see a promise of their own resilience. But they can look at yours. They can hear your story and skirt the despair when they're standing at the edge of it. Our scars can be an ugly, bright, and holy hope, if we let them be seen.

I think the greatest gift of the artist is the generosity of spirit and courage that we so often mistakenly call a willingness to be vulnerable. I believe it is only a willingness to *feel* vulnerable, because these scarred places, both inside and out, aren't areas of weakness at all but of strength. These scars and the scars of others willing to quietly show them to the similarly-wounded are not signs of our vulnerability but of our resilience. Suffering doesn't make the artist. We all suffer. And it's not the paint or the words or the guitars or the pencils that make the artist, either. It's what you do with the scars.

28.
Free Your Creativity

In bold, trendy font, the advert for some piece of computer equipment aimed at photographers and illustrators made an equally bold and trendy claim: *"Free your creativity!"*

I've seen these ads before. They must think we're a bunch of easy marks. Sell me a piece of new gear *and* free my creativity at the same time? I'm in! But free it from what, exactly?

The same tired promise of creative emancipation has been used to flog cameras and keyboards, computer applications, and bizarre novelty items, and for all I know, there are people out there selling easels and paintbrushes, guitar tuners, and the latest in pottery wheels the same way. There's more creativity in their marketing claims than will ever come as a result of these tools and toys.

We love the word *freedom*; tell me your new thing will give me freedom, and I will be all over it. You're going to free my creativity? I don't care if it costs $39 or $399, I'm in. Especially if it frees me from my fears. It does that, right?

Or the worry that I'm faking it more than others. And the fear that the world is going to find out. Or the way I constantly compare myself to others—have you got something for that?

How about the crippling anxiety that I've done my last good thing or the suspicion that even *that* wasn't all that good?

What about the procrastination? The distractions keeping me from my best work? The need to have it all figured out before I get started and therefore never gain momentum? What I wouldn't pay to be free from that!

Oh, and how about the obligations and expectations of others?

And time. Man, if I had more time, how much more creative could I be then?

How about the fear that I'm repeating myself? Or the voices that tell me I'm not good enough, even when that voice is my own? Does your thing free me from those?

What about the need for the approval of others before my work is validated?

Can your new tool help me bring greater insight or humanity to my work, or help me be more vulnerable with it? Can it help me think more in terms of possibilities and play than in terms of being correct or doing it right? Can it free me from those times I lie awake at night wondering what my next move is? No.

Because my *creativity* doesn't need to be freed; *I* do. And it won't be with toys or tools. Nor with gimmicks and platitudes. It will be freed by things that have never had a price tag, though they don't exactly come without cost.

What will truly free us is the courage to keep following our own voice, even when it's hard to hear.

We will be liberated by the faith that entertains honest doubts and, because of that, makes more honest work.

By the discipline that reaches hard for excellence but isn't seduced with unattainable ideas like perfection.

By love for the challenge and the process and the way it allows me to make my art, while in turn, my art makes me.

And by the kind of curiosity that has me peering around unfamiliar corners for the delight of discovery.

We are freed creatively not by thinking outside the boxes, because that's not where the problems are, but within them.

Creators will be freed not by our tools but by the way we think about wielding them. And, maybe most of all: why.

We will be free when we stop waiting for the muses, and neither credit nor blame them, but take responsibility for our own work while still marveling at the mystery of the unexpected and serendipitous.

We'll be free when we finally stop wasting our time, stop busying ourselves with the so-called "urgent," and get back to what's important.

And when we stop expecting everything to go well on the first try and begin instead to embrace a more evolutionary process, one that has room for the ugly first tries, the crappy first iterations, the wrong ideas, and the detours.

That would be freedom!

And most of all, perhaps, we will be free when we stop kowtowing to the need to create "content" instead of meaning, to say the *right* thing with our art (whatever that is) rather than the *safe* thing. When we stop worrying about the algorithm and start concerning ourselves with *impact*.

Creative people do not only need to be freed *from* something but *to* something. Freedom *from* is always also freedom *to*. It must be.

Freedom to make something bigger than ourselves. Freedom to open closed eyes. To ask uncomfortable questions that demand answers.

To affect change. To solve problems. To call for greater things (justice and compassion come to mind) in ways that otherwise might not be heard.

Freedom to build new and beautiful things and to rebuild those that are not.

Freedom to push this too-timid race toward courage, and to make not only those things we usually think of as creative and artistic, but freedom—with all our creativity—to make a difference. To make a change. To make light where there is none. To make a life and not just a living.

Just once, I'd like to see the ad for that.

I guess perhaps I'm hoping this book is that ad, each of the essays my attempt at selling you the idea that you can be the source of your own freedom and creative vitality, and when that fails, perhaps that we can be that for each other. What we most certainly do not need are the external things on which we too often lean: permission from others, new and better tools, perfect clarity of direction, accolades that validate our work, or the meaningless likes and other markers of approval for which we go to social media. I'm hoping that you'll see within yourself the light that illuminates your own work. Not because it's particularly bright (because it won't always be so), but because it's particularly you. There's darkness aplenty out there, and we need all the light we can find.

This is the problem with muses in the classical way of understanding them: their very externality. They represent the abdication of the very thing that makes our creative efforts so hard, but also so rewarding, and so needed: our own unique ability to respond to all that life brings by way of raw materials and do something extraordinary with them. We do not need the muses to free our creativity any more than we need new tools. We just need to show up more fully ourselves.

You are not missing pieces, nor do you lack the real tools to do your work. You're not alone in wanting to wait for inspiration before you begin, or wanting to overcome your fears first, or feeling the need to fill some gaping hole in your heart or mind, your past or your imagined future, before you do your best work. You're not alone in hearing the promise to "free your creativity" and hoping this time it might be true. Nor will you be alone in the astonishing realization, when it comes, that you don't need anything to free your creativity. *You need your creativity to free you.* It is our work that does that. Not the thing we make, not the *product* of the work, but the working itself. The putting of pen to paper and the writing of the words that have long needed to come out. The poems, rough as they are. The painting, tentative as those brush strokes appear at first. The dance, clumsy as the initial steps begin.

The great paradox of creative work (call it art or something else) is that what we make—the very making of it—also makes us.

We don't wait for freedom to create; we create to find that freedom.

We don't wait to be fearless before we make our art; we make our art to discover our courage.

We must not wait until we have the time to do these things; we must do these things to redeem our time because it's slipping away ever faster.

And we don't hope for the voices to go away before we write or sing or dance or design. We do those things to find our own voices.

About the Author

David duChemin is a best-selling author of 32 books, award-winning photographer, and leading expert in the field of creativity. His podcast and book, *A Beautiful Anarchy*, help him share his message with tens of thousands: a rich and fulfilling creative life is for everyone—not just artists.

David spent the last twelve years travelling the world as a humanitarian photographer and creativity workshop instructor on all seven continents. His adventures have taken him through winters in Russia and Mongolia and a summer on the Amazon, as well as months among nomads in the Indian Himalaya and remote Northern Kenya.

Drawing on a previous twelve-year career in comedy, David brings a dynamic and engaging presence as a presenter in workshops, on camera, or on stages for corporations like Apple and Amazon. His expertise has been profiled in magazines and podcasts including *Overland Journal, Elephant Journal* and *The Accidental Creative.*

You can find David at davidduchemin.com, on Instagram as @davidduchemin and on Facebook. His books can be found at CraftandVision.com, Amazon, and at the brick & mortar stores that would be so grateful for your patronage.

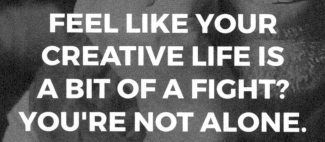

FEEL LIKE YOUR CREATIVE LIFE IS A BIT OF A FIGHT? YOU'RE NOT ALONE.

A Beautiful Anarchy is a heart-felt kick-in-the-pants podcast for everyday creators and anyone who's ever mud-wrestled with their muse. These 15-minute episodes are an honest and sensitive exploration of the joys and struggles of the creative life. Let's talk about it.

Listen on iTunes or aBeautifulAnarchy.com

CPSIA information can be obtained
at www.ICGtesting.com
Printed in the USA
BVHW081745070720
583154BV00001B/110

9 781777 220624